# Passing the Leadership Test

# Passing the Leadership Test

## *A Study Guide for the School Leaders Licensure Examination*

Leslie Jones and Eugene Kennedy

ROWMAN & LITTLEFIELD EDUCATION
A division of
ROWMAN & LITTLEFIELD PUBLISHERS, INC.
Lanham • New York • Toronto • Plymouth, UK

Published by Rowman & Littlefield Education
A division of Rowman & Littlefield Publishers, Inc.
A wholly owned subsidary of The Rowman & Littlefield Publishing Group, Inc.
4501 Forbes Boulevard, Suite 200, Lanham, Maryland 20706
www.rowman.com

10 Thornbury Road, Plymouth PL6 7PP, United Kingdom

British Library Cataloguing in Publication Information Available

**Library of Congress Cataloging-in-Publication Data**

Jones, Leslie, 1970 Oct. 5-
Passing the leadership test : a study guide for the school leaders licensure examination / Leslie Jones and Eugene Kennedy. -- 2nd ed.
p. cm.
Includes bibliographical references and index.
ISBN 978-1-61048-738-2 (cloth : alk. paper) -- ISBN 978-1-61048-739-9 (pbk. : alk. paper) -- ISBN 978-1-61048-740-5 (electronic)
1. School administrators--United States--Examinations--Study guides. 2. School administrators--Certification--United States. 3. Educational leadership--United States--Examinations--Study guides. I. Kennedy, Eugene, Ph. D. II. Title.
LB1768.J66 2012
371.20076--dc23

2012000243

The paper used in this publication meets the minimum requirements of American National Standard for Information Sciences Permanence of Paper for Printed Library Materials, ANSI/NISO Z39.48-1992.

Printed in the United States of America

# Contents

# List of Tables and Figures

## TABLES

## FIGURES

# Introduction

Preparing for a standardized test, especially a test that involves high stakes, can be a controversial enterprise. Is it cheating to study older versions of the test? Will it be helpful? Are test preparation courses legal and, if so, are they ethical? These and other questions can lead some persons to take only a passing interest in such basics as getting to know the types of questions on an examination, or reviewing the types of items presented on the examination.

Of course, a systematic strategy for preparing for a standardized test is not only ethical but is also assumed by most test publishers. Most test publishers hope that an examinee's performance will not be impaired by a lack of familiarity with the types of items on the test, paralyzing anxiety about the testing experience, or fatigue from an all-night cram session. Any of these activities, as well as many others, only cloud the inference test publishers desire to make about the level of mastery of a given examinee. Test preparation is ethical and essential.

Because test preparation is both ethical and essential, it is important to note that there are some preparation activities that are both unethical and illegal. Stealing a copy of an examination and using it to memorize correct responses is an obvious example of an illegal practice. It is not clear, however, that studying an older version of an examination and doing little else is equally inappropriate—perhaps not illegal, but almost certain to confuse the picture an examinee paints of his level of mastery of the material represented in the test.

What, then, is appropriate test preparation? This part of the book walks the reader through those activities that are appropriate and those that are not. It is intended to prepare and assist the reader, as candidates of licensure in developing a systematic plan for tackling the Educational Testing Service

School Leaders Licensure Assessment (SLLA). The specifics of the examination are presented in part II of this book. This part speaks to general principles of test preparation.

Why do some examinees do poorly on standardized tests? There are four basic reasons. First, they may simply lack sufficient mastery of the content of an examination to perform well. Most people, including developers of standardized tests, would probably agree that this is an acceptable reason for poor performance on an examination and that, in this instance, the test is functioning properly. In chapter 1, the content mastery–related difficulties some examinees experience with standardized tests are discussed.

In chapter 2, a discussion of techniques for tackling various types of test items is presented. Given the structure of the SLLA, the emphasis in this chapter is on multiple choice, essay, and constructed-response items. Another source of difficulties some examinees experience with standardized tests involves emotional states. Tests engender a certain degree of anxiety. Strategies for coping with anxiety are discussed in chapter 3. Finally, an examinee's physical state can be an impediment to maximum performance. These potential problems are addressed by the authors in the final chapter of part I of the book.

In part II of the book, specificity regarding the School Leaders Licensure Assessment (SLLA) is discussed. In chapter 5, accountability and its implications for school leaders are presented. No Child Left Behind and the reauthorization are the foci. Furthermore, the Interstate School Leaders Licensure Consortium (ISLLC) standards are argued in chapter 6. The questions on SLLA are aligned with ISLLC. In chapter 7, the nature of SLLA is covered. Sample test items are included. Multiple versions of SLLA have been administered; items from multiple versions and items for the School Superintendent Assessment are also included. In chapter 8, case studies are presented. These case studies are aligned with the ISLLC standards. They are designed to give candidates and examinees preparing for the SLLA small group practice in applying the standards. Preparing for and passing the SLLA is the immediate objective, becoming outstanding and a better prepared school is our personal vision.

This book is designed for graduate-school leadership candidates; principals and other educators serving in leadership capacities can also benefit from the book. Many states have adopted the standards of the Interstate School Leaders Licensure Consortium (ISLLC); therefore, many states have transitioned to the use of the ISLLC examination for licensure. The book provides preparation for the ISLLC examination. It presents a means of organizing and planning for the assessment that goes beyond what is currently available on the market.

*Chapter One*

# Mastery of Content

Any given standardized test is a sample of a much broader content domain. The items on a particular form represent only a small fraction of those that are conceivable. The focus of the chapter is on the mastery of the content domain sampled by a given standardized test. In the first section, assessing an individual's status on the material covered in the test is discussed. Locating and organizing information and materials to help achieve mastery is covered in the second section. In the third section, the focus is on basic principles of learning and studying. In the final section, we discuss the development of a study plan and monitoring progress towards goals and objectives.

## ASSESSING STATUS ON A CONTENT DOMAIN: KNOWING WHEN YOU KNOW AND WHEN YOU DO NOT

One of the frequently reported problems among poor learners is that they are often uncertain as to when they have achieved mastery of the material they are studying. Many report feelings of *surprise* and *frustration* at not being able to perform better on an examination when "I knew that stuff." As with most activities, the closer practice activities are to the actual performance, the more beneficial they are. With regard to testing, the problem is that an examinee's internal gauge of mastery is not keyed to the requirements of the examination. This can happen for several reasons.

First, the examinee's mastery of the material may not match the cognitive level required of the examination. For example, an examinee may focus preparation activities on recall and recognition of facts. While this is important, if the examination presents tasks which require the integration, synthesis, and application of material, the examinee in question is likely to be frustrated. This problem may be ameliorated by increasing familiarity with the kinds of tasks on the examination and systematically moving through different cognitive levels while studying (e.g., factual recall knowledge to application of knowledge in new settings).

One of the most recognized taxonomies of levels of cognitive functioning is that of Herbert Bloom. Cognitive tasks are differentiated into six hierarchical categories: knowledge, comprehension, application, analysis, synthesis, and evaluation. Whether or not the categories are hierarchical has been debated in the literature, and many other schemes for organizing cognitive tasks have been presented. For our purposes, however, it is sufficient to note that in addition to describing the different types of intellectual activities at each of the different levels, this scheme facilitates the development of appropriate items or exercises.

For example, knowledge is typically defined as the recall of factual information. There is no requirement that the examinee understand the information or be positioned to utilize it in some way, but only that the examinee simply be able to recall it as given. A question typically posed at this level is "In what year did _____ happen?" Table 1.1 presents definitions of the different levels of Bloom's taxonomy and typical question stems for each level. As part of a study plan, it can be helpful to pose questions to yourself at each of the different levels.

The World Wide Web provides an abundance of resources to help guide the reader in your understanding of Bloom's taxonomy as well as developing appropriate questions. One such resource is www.teachers.ash.org. Additionally, many "apps" have been developed to facilitate use of mobile devices (iPads, iPhones, etc.) for learning purposes. The following links summarize a small sample of the possibilities: http://ilearntechnology.com/?p=4025 and https://sites.google.com/site/bloomsapps/analyzing.

It should be noted that a second reason an examinee's self-assessment may be misleading is that it could simply be wrong. Poor learners often review material and fail to follow an initial review with an objective and representative assessment of status and accomplishments. Oftentimes they substitute a *feeling* that the material has been mastered for objective evidence of progress. Unfortunately, the intuitive feeling is more often wrong. Familiarity with basic study and learning skills can help address these difficulties. In particular, an effective study plan usually will include (a) development of self-assessments and (b) the taking of assessments developed by others.

The question stems presented in table 1.1 provide a means of developing self-assessments. Below we discuss the development of self-assessments as well as ways of locating other assessments that may help preparation activities. Toward the end of this book, we provide a series of self-assessments

Table 1.1. Definitions and Question Stems for Bloom's Taxonomy

| Cognitive Level and Definition | Sample Question Stems |
|---|---|
| *Knowledge*: The ability to recall factual information. | - In what year did ___ happen?<br>- What is the definition of ___?<br>- What examples of ___ were presented? |
| *Comprehension*: The demonstration of understanding of information by translating it, illustrating it, interpreting it, differentiating it, making predictions, and extrapolating. | - How does X differ from Y?<br>- Give an example of X. |
| *Application*: The ability to apply or use knowledge in a new situation or context. | - Use process X to solve this crisis.<br>- Discuss how product X may be used in this situation. |
| *Analysis*: The ability to dissect information into parts and demonstrate understanding of interrelationships and operating principles. | - Based on your understanding of X, what would happen in this setting if Y changed?<br>- How do the different parts of this work? |
| *Synthesis*: The ability to integrate information and formulate or produce something novel or new. | - Develop a plan to address ___. |
| *Evaluation*: The ability to use information to judge or evaluate the quality of a product, communication. | - What are the strengths & weaknesses of this ___? |

related to the ISLLC standards. In addition to the two problems noted here, there are many others. However, rather than focus on these, we consider strategies for dealing with these difficulties.

## Determining Status over a Content Domain

There are three basic parts to ascertaining one's standing relative to the content domain sampled by a standardized test. First, it is necessary to have a clear understanding of the content represented by the test in question. Second, it is necessary to actually get a sample of behavior over that content. Finally, it is important to analyze performance on the sample tests or exercises to determine areas of strengths and weaknesses.

*Step One: Diagram and Outline the Content Domain Reflected in the Examination*

The content of the SLLA is described in part II of this book. Because the content of the examination is keyed to the ISLLC standards, these standards and the knowledge, skills, dispositions, and performance indicators that they reflect should be a key part of organizing a study plan and developing or collecting self-assessments of mastery. Although described in detail in part II of this book, it is useful to summarize the content and task requirements of the SLLA here. These are presented in table 1.2.

This edition of the SLLA is a four-hour examination, divided into two sections. Section 1 is a two-hour, twenty-minute examination that consists of one hundred multiple-choice questions. As presented in the table, the items cover five content areas. Section 2 is a one-hour, forty-five-minute examination. It covers three content areas and consists of seven constructed-response items. With multiple-choice items, the goal of the examinee is to select the best option from those presented, relative to the stem of the item. For constructed-response items, the goal of the examinee is to develop the best case for his/her response that he/she can.

It is important for the examinee to remember that whether multiple choice or constructed response, the focus of the SLLA is on the examinee's mastery of the ISLLC standards. Because of the key role of the ISLLC standards in the development and evaluation of the SLLA, these standards should play a prominent role in any effort to define the content and focus of the examination. The steps in the process of defining the content and focus of the SLLA examination are as follows:

1. Collect information on the structure and focus on the examination. This is often available from test publishers, state agencies, books, articles, and other sources.
2. Collect study guides and other secondary materials that are geared to help prepare an examinee for the examination.

| Section and Topics | | Number of Items |
|---|---|---|
| Section I | Vision and goals | 18 multiple-choice items |
| | Teaching and learning | 25 multiple-choice items |
| | Managing organizational systems and safety | 15 multiple-choice items |
| | Collaborating with key stakeholders | 21 multiple-choice items |
| | Ethics and integrity | 21 multiple-choice items |
| Section II | The education system | 2 constructed-response items |
| | Vision and goals | 2 constructed-response items |
| | Teaching and learning | 3 constructed-response items |

Table 1.2. Content of the School Leaders Licensure Assessment (SLLA)

3. Collect information on the ISLLC standards. A thorough understanding of these standards is an important part of a preparation program. In part II of this publication, the standards are discussed and compared to other leadership standards.
4. As needed, collect information on specific problems identified during the study and assessment process described below.

These four steps are useful for any standardized test. In the case of the SLLA, the Educational Testing Service (ETS) website (www.ets.org/sls) provides a wealth of information relevant to the first three items:

- The School Leadership Series Test at a Glance booklet (available free of charge from the ETS website.) In this booklet, detailed examples of the questions, responses, and scoring rubrics for each of the modules of the exam are provided. Examples of responses at each of several performances levels are included.
- Reducing Test Anxiety (available free from the ETS website). Recommendations for reducing the anxiety an examinee may experience are addressed (with any of the PRAXIS series produced by ETS).
- School Leadership Series Information Bulletin (available free of charge from the ETS website). In this bulletin, information on the specifics of the exam, particularly with regard to taking the test, is presented. It is useful for preparing the examinee for the testing experience.

In addition to collecting information about the types of items and scoring criteria used on the SLLA, it is also necessary to have a thorough understanding of the ISLLC standards. Two particularly useful publications with respect to the SLLA, are as follows:

Hessel, K., & Holloway, J. (2001). *A Framework for School Leaders: Linking Standards to Practice.* Educational Testing Service: Princeton, NJ.

Sharp, W. L., Walter, J. K., & Sharp, H. M. (1998). *Case Studies for School Leaders: Implementing the ISLLC Standards.* Technomic Publishing Co.: Lancaster, PA.

Finally, the ISLLC standards as well as guidelines for professional development based on the standards are available from the Council of Chief State School Officers (www.ccsso.org).

The materials presented here provide a thorough overview of the types of tasks presented on the SLLA, the criteria used in scoring responses, and the format of the examination with respect to types of items, time limits, and so on. In addition, ISLLC-related materials provide a means of reviewing the ISLLC standards and deepening one's understanding of the implications for practice.

*Step Two: Take a Sample Test*

There is perhaps no better way to get a sense of your standing with respect to an examination than to actually take a retired or released version of the examination. It is important, however, to note that limiting preparation activities to an old exam is among the least effective ways to increase performance. However, the old exam *can* serve as a measure of your progress. It can also help you construct similar tasks and identify areas of weaknesses. Finally, it is important to simulate the examination experience as closely as possible. This means adhering to time limits, following specifications with respect to supplemental materials, and so on.

In addition, there is an ever-growing number of apps for smart phones and other mobile devices that can be enlisted to facilitate the development of items and, particularly, your ability to self-administer items organized around Bloom's or some other taxonomy (one possibility, for example, is Stick Pick). The advantage these apps offer is that they give the examinee the opportunity to practice anytime and anywhere. As is well known, as practice increases, performance normally follows.

*Step Three: Identify and Diagnose Strengths and Weaknesses*

The identification and diagnosis of weaknesses in constructed-response assessments can be more challenging than with objective types of items such as multiple-choice or true-false. Constructed-response assessments involve an objective evaluation of performance by a rater or judge. For the practice tests described above, it is likely that you, the reader, will be this judge. It will therefore be critical that your assessments be as honest and objective as possible.

It is also critical that you understand the scoring rubric. Indeed, scoring rubrics are very good tools for identifying specific areas in which your response may differ from one that receives a higher rating. It is possible and recommended to construct a bulleted list for each scoring rubric as a means of helping identify strengths and weaknesses in responses. These lists can also be related to performance indicators for the various standards, and summaries can be used to identify standard specific weaknesses.

Diagnosing weaknesses can be guided by a series of questions. Why was my response inadequate with respect to characteristics $X$ or $Y$? Was it because I lacked the knowledge, or was it because I was not able to apply or integrate it? Did I know or understand the material? Did I misunderstand the question? An obviously off-target essay is a signal of this. A less obvious sign of this is that the response may not touch on a significant number of points or issues deemed to be essential for an outstanding response. With multiple-choice items, this task is perhaps less challenging. In this instance, if an examinee selected an incorrect option, the same questions noted above can be asked until the often-subtle differences between the correct and incorrect alternatives are made clear.

Finally, rank your performance on the different parts of the examination. Begin with a series of questions as to "why?" This can be a way of identifying areas in most need. If possible, link performance to specific standards or aspects of standards. The benefit is that patterns may emerge, which can be enlightening.

## FINDING AND ORGANIZING INFORMATION

Once you have identified the areas you deem to be your weaknesses, it will be necessary to gather materials and develop an organized study plan. The materials you will need are usually found in textbooks, monographs, and scholarly articles. The key is to make rational choices and not overwhelm yourself. The tendency for many people is to start from a very basic level with the intent of working their way up through the material in a time frame that is unrealistic. This is to be avoided. A better strategy is to find out as closely as possible where you are and start from there. How, however, is one to get organized in such a way that ordered progress through material is possible?

### How to Get Organized

*Set Priorities*

Two organizational issues are in the forefront: What should be done first, and what can be done first? This is the age-old battle between practicality and goals or ambitions. Too much focus in either direction can be counterproductive. A balanced approach in which you address those things that are within your purview to tackle *and* that have significant meaning for your ultimate goals is to be preferred. A specific plan, however, is essential. A plan written on paper serves as a beacon to guide behavior and a ruler to measure progress.

For example, an examinee may observe that his responses frequently fail to be grounded in available data. It may be the case that he is uncomfortable with the statistics used or lacks experience summarizing statistical data. An obvious first issue is whether or not the examinee truly understands the statistics in question. Use and integration must wait until basic understanding is accomplished, and therefore an assessment of competence and comfort with statistics would be a first priority.

*Set Goals and Objectives That Are Realistic and Can Be Monitored*

The task should be broken down into manageable subtasks that can be addressed in a systematic manner. An objective of completing a review of a statistics textbook in an afternoon, while realistic for some, may be completely unrealistic for others. Knowing whether or not an objective is achievable within the time allotted is a key component of an effective study plan. Unrealistic goals lead to frustration and can negatively impact effort.

Objectives should be monitored. This depends heavily on the level of specificity of their wording. An objective like "study a basic statistic text" is ambiguous. To study can mean any number of different things. A more specific objective would focus on actions such as "read the statistics text and pass (80 percent correct) the end-of-chapter examination." This provides a basis for monitoring progress (Was the text read during the period of time specified?) and evaluating status (Was the goal of 80 percent correct achieved?).

## Locating Help

In addition to libraries, there are many resources on the World Wide Web that can help greatly with preparation activities. Additionally, many associations offer short courses, some of which are online.

## STUDY, LEARNING, AND DISCIPLINED PROGRESS

People have a variety of preferences in terms of how they acquire and process information. These preferences and habits are grouped into so-called learning styles. There has emerged a large body of literature focused on different learning styles, with the goal being to encourage educators to incorporate different learning styles into their instruction. The evidence, however, suggests that efforts to do so have not yielded significant improvements in achievement. In part, this may stem from the fact that most individuals have a variety of learning preferences and that these may change over time or evolve for particular situations. There is, it seems, no right style for any individual. What seems to work best is probably the most useful approach to the idea of learning preferences. Some of the distinctions that have been drawn include the following:

*Verbal and Graphic Presentations.* Some individuals prefer verbal communications as opposed to written or some other method of transmittal. These individuals may grow bored easily when asked to read a long paragraph or sort through a book chapter for answers to some questions. Alternatively, these same persons may find graphic depictions or spoken presentations to be especially illuminating, engaging, and retained for long periods of time. The clear implication is that if studying material, it makes sense for these persons to organize or even create for example graphic depictions and verbal notes.

*Isolated versus Social Situations.* Some persons prefer to engage material in the context of a high-stimulus environment. These persons may prefer to work in coffee shops, open meeting areas, or other social gatherings. The noise and other external stimuli may help keep these individuals focused and engaged with the material they are studying. In contrast, some persons are most effective when they reduce the amount of noise or other stimuli in the environment. The implication is that while one approach may seem "absurd" to some, it unquestionably works for others.

These are but a few examples of different preferences individuals have for "how" they learn. The key point is that there is no one right answer. What may work for one individual may absolutely not work for another. A reasonable approach may begin with self reflection and a personal assessment to determine "what works best for me". Logically following self and personal assessment is sharpening of study skills, development of a personal study plan, and implementation of it.

## Study Skills

Study skills include those behaviors that facilitate the learning of material. They involve reading at a rate and with a level of recall and comprehension to acquire needed information in a timely manner. They include note taking, summarizing activities, and review activities that permit access to learned material over extended periods of time.

## Some Signs Your Study Skills May Need Improvement

Some of the more obvious signs of inadequate study skills include the following:

- Inability to recall needed material
- Inability to comprehend or understand material presented in a verbal, written, or other form
- Chaotic and disorganized files, notes, and records that inhibit review

# HOW TO STUDY

## Adopt a Positive Attitude

As with most activities, the attitude one brings to a task can have a significant impact on the likelihood of success. Students who approach written material with an attitude of disinterest, hostility, or helplessness are more likely to have a frustrating learning experience than those with more positive attitudes. Positive reinforcement of previous achievement or simply repeating positive statements about one's ability to effectively tackle a task is a demonstrated way of enhancing performance.

Visualization of success and the sequence of steps needed to achieve it have also been shown to promote success. The point is that the attitude a person brings to a task will affect behavior and performance on the task. This is true in general and certainly applies to preparation for the SLLA and efforts to study and master related material.

## Time Management

Knowing how to manage time and mental resources is a problem for most people but is very common among students who struggle in school. Time is managed most effectively by assigning certain activities to specific slots of time. The assignment process needs to be such that things can be done within the time frame specified, and the overall allocation of time should be realistic and responsive to habits and other obligations. For example, saying that you will read from 6:00 to 8:00 p.m., when family obligations are likely to compete, is unrealistic and can lead to frustration.

Similarly, planning to read for six consecutive hours when past performance clearly shows a tendency to effectively read and sit in one place for a maximum of two hours is simply preparing to fail. The point is that the development of a plan to allocate time and energy should be realistic and designed to achieve desired objectives. Also, it is important to include time for breaks and other rewards to ameliorate boredom and a wandering mind. Finally, it is essential to monitor time use. This can reveal patterns of unusual productivity or obvious lack of productivity. A realistic time management plan will involve responsiveness to current realities and future goals and objectives.

## A Place to Study

Humans have the habit of associating certain types of behaviors with specific places. While it is certainly possible for certain places to serve many functions and for different functions to be done in multiple locations, with regard to study activities and the mental tasks associated with them, it is likely that most individuals have developed specific habits. Some are capable of greater concentration during the morning hours and in spaces that are far removed from noise and other distractions.

On the other hand, some individuals prefer to be in wide-open spaces and in the midst of a great deal of activity. The point is that there is no best place to study that fits everyone. An effective study plan calls for finding those circumstances (time of day, days of week, place) that facilitate your ability to consume and process significant amounts of information. This may require a bit of trial and error, but the old adage applies here: if it works for you, stay with it.

## Set Specific Objectives

This was mentioned above in the context of organization and planning, but it bears repeating here. A study session should have specific objectives so that at the end of the session, it is possible to determine whether or not the effort was successful. In addition, specific goals and objectives promote consistency of effort and help combat the tendency for "unscheduled breaks" and other interruptions to take one off target.

## Include Rewards

While it is true that effective study is dependent on cognitive skills, it is also true that the effort needed to improve study habits is largely a psychological phenomenon. As mentioned above, focusing on the positive is a way of increasing the likelihood that effort will increase. It is also true that positive reinforcement of success helps sustain effort. A successful study session should be followed by a reward. This could be something as simple as listening to a record, enjoying a snack, or some other activity you value. The result of linking the two is that there is likely to be a positive impact on your efforts to have successful study sessions in the future.

## Read, Relate, Review

To improve understanding and retention of written material, it is necessary to act on the material in some way. This can be as simple as posing questions as you read through a passage: "Can this be right?" "How does this relate to what I know or believe?" "How does this compare with what was presented earlier?" "What is the primary point the author is trying to make?" These or similar questions engage you with the written material and require that you access your personal knowledge base and cognitive processes that interact with the material. The result is that more connections to previous knowledge are established, and memory and recall of key points are improved.

Review is also an important part of effective study. Reviewing material you have read provides a means of pulling the pieces together, especially if you have taken notes during the process. It helps learners formulate the "big picture." It is this perspective that the learner will, through repeated use, retain and be more readily apply. And it is the big picture that will usually key the learner to specifics.

## Take Notes

Taking notes is an important part of an effective study plan. The act of taking notes forces the learner to summarize and connect facts and specifics. Well-organized notes also provide a means for the learner to "relive" the experience of the material and renew familiarity with it. Notes should not be so specific as to be a reproduction of written material. Instead, they should be summaries or restatements of key points. They should follow the presentation and be accurate as to what was presented. Mobile apps for taking notes and creating flash cards are available for most devices and should be considered as part of the overall plan.

## Apply, Teach, and Assess

Students who use acquired knowledge are more likely to be able to retain and extend it than those who do not. Information simply imparted and left idle vanishes quickly and is least likely to be retained and extended. Because of this fact, it is important for students to use new information. The structure of the SLLA promotes this in that it focuses on applications of ISLLC standards to situations likely to be encountered by school principals and principal candidates. A logical part of a study plan, therefore, is to make a concerted effort to apply new material to realistic problems.

Most people reading this text will have had considerable experience in schools. As a result, it should not be too difficult for the reader to conceive of a scenario in which material reviewed for the SLLA can be applied. The act of applying this material will have the benefit of strengthening its connections to current knowledge and will increase the likelihood that it will be reflected in a written response to one of the SLLA prompts or recalled when confronted with a multiple-choice item.

Another effective way of solidifying new information is to teach it to others. The act of teaching requires an individual to organize information, develop connections and examples of how that information relates to current knowledge, and prepare a script for presentation so as to promote learning. Teaching is a very effective way of acquiring and deepening understanding. Because some readers of this text will not have the opportunity to teach this material, developing lesson plans can serve as a close approximation.

Assessing mastery of new material is an essential part of an effective study plan. When available, examinations included in textbooks at the end of chapters present a good opportunity to assess understanding. Similarly, many publishers will have student study guides and related materials that can be used to self-assess mastery. Finally, when these options are not available, it is appropriate for the learner to develop his/her own assessment.

To be most effective, this may be taken after a period of time has passed between when the exam was prepared and taken. The value of an objective assessment of mastery, however, cannot be overemphasized. It was noted earlier in this chapter that many poor learners often fail to appreciate their lack of mastery. This is often the case because no efforts to obtain an objective assessment were made.

Recommendations in this book have evolved since the first edition. Similarly, in recent years a number of web-based resources have also been developed. Many are free and can be downloaded. Some present organizational templates, some involve time managers, and so on. A review and sample of these possibilities can be found at the following link: http://newtonassistive-tech.wikispaces.com/Resources+for+Study+Skills,+Organization,
    +Note-Taking+and+Research.

## CONCLUSION

In this chapter, a short overview of the steps needed to take a systematic approach to preparation of the SLLA was presented. The essential parts to development of a plan involved understanding the assessment and mastering the content domain reflected in the assessment. Various techniques were offered for accomplishing these steps. The reader should, from this chapter, develop a plan with specific timelines, goals, and objectives. The plan should be dynamic in that as new information about status over the domain and performance on the examination is obtained, the study, learning, and review process changes. The next chapter deals more specifically with the types of items found on the SLLA.

*Chapter Two*

# Understanding and Preparing for the Format of Standardized Tests

As most of us know all too well, the format of standardized tests has undergone significant changes in recent years. The standardized tests most examinees confronted in the 1970s and 1980s consisted largely of multiple-choice and true-false items. Most examinations have changed drastically. The perennial standardized test, the SAT, or Scholastic Aptitude Test, for example, had more than a token number of open-ended math items included in its March 2005 administration. These changes reflect the desire of test developers to present examinees with a varied set of opportunities to demonstrate their proficiency over a content domain.

The changes in the SAT are part of a broader trend that has seen almost all standardized testing programs in the K–16 educational setting move away from sole reliance on multiple-choice or so-called objective-item formats. Most of these tests now include items that require examinees to provide a written response. These are variously called open-ended items, constructed-response items, and performance assessments. These items require an examinee to (a) read a prompt, (b) review and digest background material, (c) formulate and organize a response, and (d) write the response so that a reviewer can read it. As such, they are believed by many to be able to tap higher-order thinking skills in a way that is difficult to accomplish with true-false or multiple-choice items.

It is also the case, however, that an examinee who blunders on one of these tasks, despite familiarity with the content of the examination, will likely not receive the full credit possible for a given item. Open-ended items are more complex than traditional multiple-choice items, and comfort with this format is an important part of an examinee's overall performance.

As noted above, while the items on the SLLA are mostly multiple-choice, there are seven that are of the constructed-response variety. In the first part of this chapter, the focus is on the multiple-choice item format; the focus is on the constructed-response format in the second part of this chapter.

# THE MULTIPLE-CHOICE ITEM

The multiple-choice item has been around for decades. The basic structure is that of a stem, which presents a problem situation or question, and a series of answers, one of which is best or correct. The others are called distracters because their function is to appeal to and distract the less knowledgeable examinee. The examinee's task is to select the option that best addresses the problem posed in the stem, a process which requires that distracters be eliminated. The difficulty of a multiple-choice item lies in the distracters. There are a variety of different types of distracters that appear on many standardized tests.

## The True but Irrelevant Distracter

These distracters present the examinee with a fact that is perhaps related and true, but not an appropriate response to the stem of the item. For example, a stem might pose the question, "Who was the first president of the United States?" A true but irrelevant distracter might be "Abraham Lincoln." The less knowledgeable examinee might recognize this person as a U.S. president but not be able to recall the fact that he was not the first president. Focusing on the problem presented in the stem can be a useful way of avoiding the appeal of a true but irrelevant distracter.

## Common Misconceptions

Common misconceptions are beliefs, folklore, and the like that are held to be true but in fact are not. They often represent misconceptions students formulate as they are trying to master a concept. These are often collected from students during the training process and appear as options on multiple-choice items. The only effective strategy to counter a common misconception is to possess a sound understanding of the content.

## None of the Above and All of the Above

These options are somewhat rare on multiple-choice items. They present the examinee with the task of deciding whether none of the other options presented is correct or whether all of the other options are correct. One exception to either one automatically eliminates these as effective distracters, and they are therefore less often seen than options that focus on content.

In addition to this basic structure, there are many varieties of multiple-choice items. Some present graphs, tables, or scenarios and require the examinee to study the external material, consider the options provided, and select the one that best addresses the goal or criteria specified in the stem. Alternatively, the examinee may be asked to select the best two or three options of those provided. In either case, the types of external material presented for these varieties is similar to what is typically presented along with open-ended or constructed-response questions.

### THE CONSTRUCTED-RESPONSE ITEM

The constructed response item requires an examinee to (a) read a prompt, (b) review and digest background material, (c) formulate and organize a response, and (d) write the response so that a reviewer can read it. In this section of the chapter, we review each of these tasks in turn. The objective of this section is to familiarize the reader with these acts so that they become second nature when the SLLA is taken.

## Reading the Prompt

There are three basic parts to an open-ended item. These are (a) the situation or scenario, (b) response instructions, and (c) background materials. Effective reading of a prompt means having a sound idea of the facts presented in the prompt and knowing what is required in a response. How does one get a sound idea of the facts in a prompt? The answer is to know the who, what, when, how, and why of the prompt. In other words, who did what? When? Why? And how was it accomplished? Consider, for example, the following:

> Bill Smith, an eighth-grade teacher, was accused of striking a boy during the lunch hour. The incident was not reported to the principal until several days after it reportedly happened. It was mentioned by one of the school custodians in a casual conversation with the principal. The tone of the conversation suggested that the incident was of little significance and not likely to be known by many people. How, as principal, would you respond?

Who? Who are the players in this scenario? They are the custodian, an unnamed child, the eighth-grade teacher, Bill Smith, and the school principal.

What happened? We do not know whether or not Bill Smith actually struck a student. We only know that the custodian reported this. We also do not know whether the custodian was a witness to the alleged incident or is simply repeating something he/she heard. What we know with certainty is that the custodian reported this incident to the principal.

How? The fact that the conversation between the principal and the custodian was casual seems significant. The scenario points this out, possibly, so as to alert the reader to something worthy of note. At this point, however, the reader does not know what is implied. This might become relevant later. For example, this statement may suggest a potential problem if the item also presents information on the discipline records of teachers in the school and Mr. Smith's record appears somehow unusual.

Perhaps there is an unusual number of visits to the school nurse from students in his class. This, in conjunction with the custodian's tone, suggests that something may have happened and that it may not be an isolated event. However, this is just conjecture and needs a process for exploration or additional data. The important point is that a subtle clue is perhaps presented in the "how" of the communication.

When? The only reference to anything temporal in the prompt is the fact that the incident was not reported until several days after it allegedly occurred. Was it a well-kept secret? If so, what does this imply about the flow of information in the school? Does it imply something about the principal's lines of communication with faculty and students? The possibilities are many, and as more information is presented, it should become clear to the careful reader what the key issues are. Recall from an earlier discussion that there are many correct responses to open-ended items. However, all correct responses will have certain similarities, which are reflected in the scoring key.

Why? The final question to pose to a prompt is the why of the events. Why, for example, was this not reported earlier? Why did it not come from a student or someone who actually saw the incident, if indeed it happened? Interestingly, the motivations of the custodian in telling this to the principal, as presented in prompt, seem innocent and almost trivial.

The questions outlined above provide an examinee with a means of chronicling and organizing the key events and facts presented in a prompt. There is, of course, a danger of overanalyzing any particular aspect of a prompt. Thus it is important to read the prompt completely and then make simple, brief notes. Notes that are too detailed and specific can quickly become an obstacle and hinder performance.

## Knowing What Is Required in a Response

The second important set of facts an examinee should take away from a prompt is a clear idea of what is required in a response. Some open-ended items are very specific about this. They will include terms similar to the following: describe, compare and contrast, defend, explain, and so on. They may also point to specific elements that should be addressed in the response. For example, "Your response should be no longer than one page, and be sure to list the five components of _____ and explain how each supports the course of action you will take." Finally, some open-ended items will even give the examinee guidance as to how responses will be evaluated. For example, "Your response will be evaluated on (a) accuracy, (b) logical consistency, (c) sentence structure and grammar, . . ." and so on.

Of course, it is likely that the prompt will not be as specific as to outline and structure the response. This is often left up to the examinee and will require some familiarity with key terms or phrases. The following presents several of the more common "action" terms in open-ended items and suggestions for ways of tackling them.

## Compare and Contrast

These items require the examinee to compare one course of action with another, one item with another, one event with another, and so on. The point at which many examinees fail an item of this nature is that they either (a) do not actually compare A with B or (b) they compare A and B on irrelevant criteria. The following, for example, is not a comparison of two classes, but descriptions of different aspects of each:

> Class A. There are thirteen students in Ann's class. Ten are girls; and three are boys. All speak fluent Spanish.
> Class B. The children in class B are very well behaved. They rarely make noise during class transitions and almost never disturb the classrooms around them.

To avoid this, it is best to identify the specific traits on which the comparisons will be based at the start and follow a strict plan for the presentation. Some of the more common bases on which comparisons are made include the following:

• financial costs to organization;
• time and effort required to institute policy;
• potentially negative consequences if the effort fails;
• possible unanticipated consequences;
• benefits to making the change; and
• likelihood of success.

For example, consider the problem of an ineffective teacher. Two courses of action are presented, fire the teacher or require that she undergo retraining.
   Financial costs if the teacher is fired include

- the salary requirements of a new teacher;
- costs of conducting a search; and
- costs of substitutes.

Financial costs of retraining the teacher include

- costs of the required workshops; and
- costs of substitutes during the time the training will occur.

Social costs of firing the teacher include

- impact on teacher morale; and
- impact on student morale.

Of course, the lists could go on. The point is that the criteria on which the comparisons are based are explicitly stated, and the presentation of the comparisons is structured so that it keeps the examinee on task and makes it easy for the grader or reviewer to follow the response.

*Evaluate*

Items that require the examinee to evaluate a course of action are similar to the compare and contrast, but in this instance the comparison is against a body of literature, ideas, or practices, and the objective is to paint a picture of how a particular action may appear from that perspective. For example, the idea that every child can learn is a theme present throughout the ISLLC standards. Suppose, then, that during a school start-up assembly the principal were to make the following statement: "We expect great things from our smart students. But, for those who just do not have the machinery for school work, well, we want you to try as hard as you can, but not to hurt yourselves."
   The obvious implication of this statement is that not all students can learn. If asked to evaluate this statement, an examinee might start by pointing out the inconsistency of this statement with the ISLLC standards. He/she could then reference research which suggests that the climate of this statement and the low expectations it communicates are both linked to poor outcomes for students and poorly functioning schools. The point is that the examinee tries to depict this statement from the vantage point of a specific body of literature.

*Discuss*

Items that ask an examinee to discuss a position, incident, or event are typically focused on the examinee's ability to analyze a set of circumstances. For example, can the examinee explain the sequence of events leading up to a particular incident from the vantage point of the literature and known "best practices"? Do they understand the advantages and disadvantages of a particular position as it is talked about in a particular body of literature or research? What can an examinee say about likely future developments regarding a specific policy? These questions require that an examinee carefully outline the position, incident, or event relative to a body of literature. For example, consider the following scenario:

> Dave Brown, the football coach, teaches social studies during the third period. The students in his class consistently score lower on the social studies section of the statewide test than any other group in the school. The principal met Coach Brown and recommended that he attend a workshop on instructional strategies. He did, and the performance of his students increased. Unfortunately, the record of the football team grew steadily worse, and much of the blame was placed on the principal. Discuss this sequence of events. What would you recommend to the principal and why?

To respond to this item, examinees must be able to explain the events chronicled in the scenario as to how they might logically relate to one another. For example, it may be the case that Coach Brown may have had little experience in the classroom prior to being assigned the third-period social studies class and as a result, his efforts to improve necessarily took away from the time he could devote to coaching. It is possible that the worsening record of the football team could have far-reaching negative consequences for the entire school internally and in relation to the community. These, of course, would be factors to consider in planning a response strategy. The essential point is that an adequate response to this item requires consideration of the causes of the event and the future consequences of different courses of action (remove the coach from the classroom; get him an assistant; take no action).

## Review and Digest Background Material

Background material may take any form, but the most common are (a) text, (b) graphs, and (c) tables. In constructed-response items, there will almost always be more material presented than is actually needed for the response. It is the examinee's task to sort through the material and identify that which is useful. After sorting the material it is necessary to locate the specific bits of information needed for a response. All of this can be facilitated if the material is approached in a purposeful way.

That is, if the material is queried for specific issues, it is easier to sort through it, organize it, and make sense of it. This is in sharp contrast to scanning or reviewing material without any preset structure. As noted above, the problem scenario and response instructions should help the examinee to structure his/her review activities, alerting him/her to the kinds of additional data that might be relevant for the problem at hand. In the following section, we focus on (a) organizing material for review, (b) summarizing the content, and (c) extracting information from different types of material.

*Organizing Material for Review*

The first step is to always determine what has been provided. It the list is long, then generate a short summary. For example, if the problem is focused on an instructional issue with a teacher, the following background material might be organized into the following categories:

• supervisor evaluations from past three years;
• classroom observations from a district;
• classroom-level results on standardized tests;
• student-level results on standardized tests;
• discipline-related summaries; and
• samples of classroom materials.

Within any of these categories, there may be subcategories of materials. Further, there may be data for multiple years. What this list will accomplish is to give the examinee a quick and brief overview of the material. It then becomes easier to interact with the material to locate relevant information.

*Summarize Content*

This simply refers to the need to formulate a brief summary of the information that is provided. For example, the student-level results on standardized tests category may contain student score reports. A quick summary might simply list the types of data presented:

• ethnicity, gender, age, disability code, lunch status;
• standard scores, national percentile rank, normal curve equivalent, stanine; and
• school-level percentile rank, district-level percentile rank.

## Extracting Information from Different Types of Background Material

Examinees differ in their ability to quickly identify and summarize key information presented in textual, graphic, and tabular formats. The following sections offer guidelines for each of these categories.

### Dealing with Background Text Material

The difficulties examinees have with text material often stem from basic problems with reading comprehension and the inability to summarize textual material. These, of course, are basic study skills, but they warrant quick review in this text. The following suggestions are offered:

*Locate the Big Idea.* A good first step in approaching textual material is to locate the big ideas. What is the title? Is there a content outline? If so, what does it suggest in terms of what will be presented? These and similar questions give the reader a good overview of the purpose and content of the material.

A useful next step is to actually scan the material. If several chapters are presented, again locating the subheadings and other minor headings gives the reader the ability to anticipate the presentation and interact with the material. Interacting with the material is a good way of increasing reading comprehension. Finally, develop a summary of the key ideas presented. Summaries may be as simple as a bulleted list or an annotated outline.

*Increase Reading Speed.* This is useful for extraneous material or material with which you have some familiarity. To increase the rate at which you traverse this material, try the following:

- avoid reading word by word. Increase "perceptual scan" to include groups of words;
- reduce the need to vocalize words to gain comprehension;
- rely on selective remembering of what was read;
- avoid rereading material on a page;
- adjust the rate for the type of material and the purpose for reading it; and
- scan the material, focusing on a few key ideas.

Of course, if you require more detail and/or the material is difficult or unfamiliar, you should slow your rate and focus on understanding what is being presented.

*Rehearse and Review.* Review what you have read. Mentally rehearse the big ideas and the key points you have been able to identify. This will help the material become more meaningful and assist you in your efforts to summarize it and access it.

*Take Notes.* Take notes on what you have read. Start with the big ideas and then summarize the key points you have been able to locate.

*Dealing with Background Graphic Material*

Many different types of graphs are used to present educational data. Some of the more common ones are pie charts, line graphs, and bar charts. The data in these graphs can be numbers or percentages.

Figure 2.1 presents a typical pie chart. The size of the slice of the pie for each teacher is proportional to the percent of his/her third-grade class that achieved a passing score on the exam. The data is reflected in the chart. Some of these charts will have the percentages printed in a legend or in the pie. A quick way for an administrator to get a sense of which class has the highest passing rate is presented in this chart. For these data, Ms. Jones has the class with the largest passing rate. It is worth noting that this information alone does not assure the administrator that the quality of instruction in this class was superior to that of the others. Information on the entry characteristics of the other classes would be needed before such a conclusion could be approached. Documentation on the exact techniques used in the different classes would be viable data to have accessible.

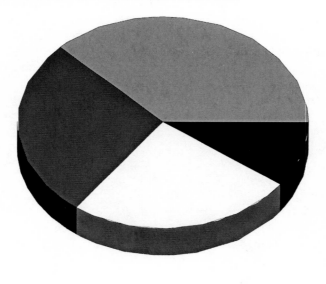

Ms. Jones        Ms. Roberts
Mr. Smith        Ms. Wilson

Figure 2.2 presents a typical line graph seen in educational publications. The data presented in the figure represents achievement rates for different third-grade classes over a four-year period. The data clearly shows a good deal of variation for the class taught by Ms. Jones. They also show that Mr. Wilson's classes have shown steady growth over the four-year period represented in the graph.

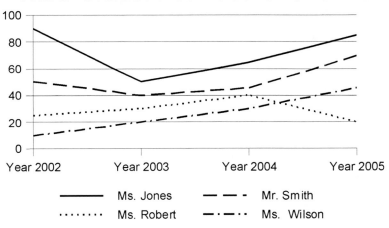

A typical bar chart of educational data is presented in figure 2.3. The data for the four teachers in the other graphs is presented for each year of four years. The data clearly show that the students in Ms. Jones's class outperform the other third graders.

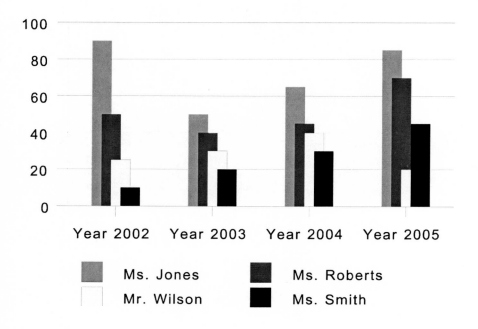

*Dealing with Background Tabular Material*

Most educators have some degree of experience with data presented in tables. If they encounter difficulties, they usually stem from (a) problems with knowing which data elements are relevant or (b) understanding the data that are presented. This latter problem is the focus of this discussion. In particular, we focus on the meaning of various statistical and measurement data often presented in educational tables and reports.

*Understanding Statistical Terms*. There are three classes of statistics commonly used in educational reports: central tendency, dispersion, and position. We discuss each of these in turn.

*Central tendency*. As the term suggests, central tendency is concerned with locating the typical or average point in a set of data. This could be the average test score for a group of students, the average salary of classroom teachers, or the average number of fans at a sporting event. There are many different ways of determining the average for a data set. Three measures of central tendency are common in education: the mean, the median, and the mode.

The one most familiar to educators is the *mean*. If we let $X$ represent the score of a student on a classroom test, then the sample mean, $\chi = \sum / N$, where N is the total number of students and $\sum$ signifies that we sum the scores of all students in the class. The mean uses all students in the class to compute an average. Because of how the mean is computed, it is vulnerable to unusual observations. For example, if one particularly gifted reader were added to a class for remedial readers, the mean reading level of the class could suggest that the remedial readers are performing at an acceptable level. In fact, this would be misleading.

Because of restrictions of the sample mean, the *median* is sometimes preferred over the mean as a measure of central tendency. The median is defined as the score in a distribution that divides the distribution into two equal parts. For example, if there were five students in a class and their scores were 2, 3, 6, 8, and 11, the median would be 6 because it divides the distribution into two equal parts. The median does not use all of the observations in a set of data and is therefore less sensitive to unusual observations. To follow up on the example earlier, a gifted reader would not dramatically affect the median in a classroom of remedial readers. It is also important to point out that the median is appropriate for ranks, such as those for high-school students.

The final measure of central tendency considered is the *mode*. This is simply the value that occurs with the greatest frequency. In the scores 2, 2, 3, 4, and 5, 2 is the mode because it occurs twice in the distribution and other values occur once. The median is 3—refer to the discussion in the previous paragraph.

*Dispersion.* Another important characteristic of a data set is the amount of variation or dispersion in the data. If all of the observations in a data set are equal, then there is no variation. However, this is rare, and for most characteristics of interest in education, there is some degree of variation. There are many statistics designed to reflect the amount of variation in a set of data. The ones most frequently reported in the education literature are the range, interquartile range, variance, and standard deviation.

The *range* is simply the difference between the largest and smallest scores. Most classroom-level score reports will present the minimum and maximum scores in an effort to give the reader some sense of the range of performance for a class. Because the range is based on extreme scores, it tends to be sensitive to fluctuations. It is also the case that it is based on only two observations in a data set. The amount of variation in two distributions could vary dramatically in the middle of a scale, yet if their minimum and maximum scores were identical, the range would indicate that they have the same degree of variation.

The *interquartile* range is a measure of variability based on outlying scores, but in this instance, the extreme minimum and maximum scores are not used. Instead, the interquartile range is defined as the difference between the score that divides the upper 25 percent of a distribution and the score that divides the bottom 25 percent of a distribution. It is considered to be more stable than the range and represents the amount of dispersion of the middle 50 percent of a distribution.

The *variance* is a very common measure of dispersion. It can be defined as the average squared deviations from the sample mean. The basic logic is that the difference between each score and the sample mean is obtained and squared. These values are then averaged. If there is considerable variation in the data, the variance will have a large value. If there is little or no variation in a set of data, the variance will be nearly zero. The variance uses all of the data in a distribution and is therefore susceptible to extreme observations.

The *standard deviation* is a measure of dispersion based on the variance. Because the variance is defined in terms of squared deviation units, the standard deviation is obtained by taking the square root of the variance. It is an attempt to generate a measure of dispersion that can be interpreted with reference to the original scale of the data. It can be interpreted as the typical distance of a score from the mean of the sample.

*Understanding Key Measurement Terms.* There are a number of key terms in measurement any educator should be familiar with as well. These terms include those related to the validity and reliability of scores and those related to different types of scores.

*Validity* is concerned with the question of whether or not a scale measures that which it intends. *Reliability* is concerned with the extent to which errors of measurement affect scores or the classification of individuals based on their scores. Traditionally, validity has been classified into different types: criterion-related validity evidence, content-related evidence, and construct-related validity evidence.

Criterion-related evidence of validity concerns the extent to which test scores correlate with some known criterion performance. A score is considered if it has an expected relationship with some valued criterion measure. Content-related evidence is concerned with the extent to which tests accurately reflect the content intended. Finally, construct-related evidence of validity concerns the degree to which evidence supports the use of tests as measures of some underlying psychological construct.

Contemporary authors consider the distinctions to be superfluous and hold that all the distinctions fall under the umbrella of construct validity. Nevertheless, it is important to be familiar with these and related terms. The two other validity terms most commonly encountered in the literature are instructional validity and curricular validity. Instructional validity refers to the match between a test and the instruction that was given. Curricular validity refers to the extent to which an examination matches a curriculum.

Reliability is most often reported for entire tests or subtests. Reliability coefficients range from 0, meaning that a score is seriously impacted by errors of measurement, to 1.0, meaning that there is little error present. Most professionally prepared educational tests have values in the vicinity of .90 or greater. A related measurement statistic is the standard error of measurement. This value is used to place a band around the score of an individual examinee and reflects the range of possible values of his true (with errors of measurement) performance.

There are numerous *standard scores* used in education. Some of the more common include the following:

- Stanine scores arestandard scores that have a mean of 5 and a standard deviation of 2.
- Normal curve equivalents are standard scores that have a mean of 50 and a standard deviation of 21.06.
- Grade equivalents are standard scores designed to reflect the grade level at which an examinee is functioning.

*Position.* Measures of position are common to educators. These include percentiles, deciles, quartiles, and the like. They help bring meaning to a score by allowing the user to interpret the score in reference to a comparison group of individuals. For example, a percentile rank of 67 means that 67 percent of the individuals in the comparison group scored at or below this point.

Deciles, unlike percentile, divide a distribution into ten equal units. Quartiles divide a distribution into four equal parts.

It is important for anyone interpreting percentiles to keep in mind that they are not equal interval measures. That is, the distance, with reference to the underlying distribution between percentiles of 1 and 10, is not the same as the distance between percentiles of 51 and 60. Similarly, it is important to keep in mind that the percentile, decile, or quartile gets its meaning from the comparison group. In measurement literature, these are often referred to as norms. It is important to make sure the norm or comparison group is similar to the group being compared and that they are current. Finally, a distinction can also be drawn between group norms and individual norms. Group norms are less variable than individual norms and should be used when comparisons are at the group level.

## Formulating, Organizing, and Writing a Coherent Response

The following suggestions are offered as aids in helping formulate and present a coherent response.

- Outline the requirements of the item and address each one. This prevents you from falling into the trap of a response that is off target.

- Organize your response in a coherent and logical flow of ideas. It is not sufficient to simply list key points. The difference between a good and average response is often whether important points are integrated in such a way as to show that an examinee understands the material.
- Always have a topic sentence. The topic sentence serves to alert the reader of your response as to its organization and major focus.

As an example, consider the following scenario:

> Ms. Jones, the third-grade teacher, has brought a single student to your office every day for the past two weeks. She reports that the student is disrespectful and the student responds that Ms. Jones does not like him. How do you respond?

Response One: The following represents a poorly organized response:

- collect data on previous behavior problems of the student;
- collect data on previous classroom management practices of Ms. Jones;
- interview the student; and
- interview Ms. Jones.

Response Two: The following represents a response that is organized better:

> The persistence of this problem suggests that a more thorough approach be taken than has been taken in the past. Toward this end, my response would involve (a) collection of relevant data, (b) analysis of the collected data, and (c) formulation of several hypotheses and possible solution strategies.
> The driving principle for my data collection activities would be to obtain a complete and balanced view of the problem and its antecedents. For example, I would not only carefully interview the student, but I would also interview Ms. Jones. The questions posed would attempt to describe the setting leading up to the confrontation, the sequence of events, and the response of both parties.

The greater organization, detail, and integration of the second response suggests that the examinee has a greater depth of understanding. A reviewer of the first response is left to wonder whether the examinee has little more than surface knowledge of the material, which is usually a sign of memorization of factual information.

## GENERAL GUIDELINES FOR TAKING OPEN-ENDED EXAMINATIONS

This section lists some of the more well-recognized strategies for dealing effectively with constructed-response items:

## Read and Follow Directions

- Read the instructions carefully.
- Know how much time you have to work on a particular section of the exam.
- Know how many items are included in a given section.
- Do a quick scan of any material that accompanies a particular section.

## Manage Time

- Remember that your response to an open-ended item requires that you organize and write a response. Be sure to leave time for both activities. Below, we suggest that you outline the key points in your response. This can help you maintain control of your presentation and makes it easier for you to monitor your progress.
- Plan how you will use your time.
- Monitor your effort on given parts of the exam so that you do not run out of time.
- Leave time for review and editing.

## Answer Each Item, Even If You Only Have Partial Knowledge

- If you have no clue as to how to respond to an item, jot down your initial ideas and leave it for later. Chances are, your initial ideas will be somewhere in the ballpark of the correct response.
- Do not simply leave an item blank. A blank response removes any possibility of partial credit.

## Review Your Answers

- Read your responses, paying close attention to the flow of ideas, grammar, and other distractions that may take away from your response and/or make it difficult for a reviewer to understand what you have written.

## Be Attentive to Key Words

- Open-ended items usually include key words that should alert the examinee to the type of response required. These include compare/contrast, discuss, and evaluate. These terms were discussed above.

## GENERAL GUIDELINES FOR TAKING MULTIPLE-CHOICE EXAMINATIONS

The following general guidelines for answering multiple-choice items are offered:

- Read the stem carefully and be sure you fully understand the question it poses.
- If you are confident in your response, find the option that best fits what you know to be true.
- If you are less certain of your response than implied above, start a process of eliminating options. Some are usually easy to eliminate, and others may require a bit of reflection.
- Work as rapidly as possible, and return to items that are more challenging than others.

## CONCLUSION

In this chapter, we discussed the variety of items an examinee will find on the SLLA. While the majority is of the multiple-choice variety, the current version of this exam also includes constructed response items. Strategies for dealing with these formats, especially when they include reference materials (e.g., maps, statistics, etc.), are discussed. General guidelines are offered.

*Chapter Three*

# Test Anxiety and Your Emotions

Excessive anxiety about the testing experience can be a debilitating and humiliating experience. It can happen before, during, and even after an examination. The first two scenarios, obviously, pose the greatest threat to actual performance. Anxiety may appear in the form of mental blocks and an inability to cognitively engage material. It may lead to avoidance behavior, such as procrastination or mental flights of fantasies that consume large amounts of time but yield little progress with regard to preparation for an exam or actual performance.

Excessive anxiety can have negative physical and emotional outcomes, such as a loss of sleep or appetite, uncontrolled nervousness, and depression. Unchecked, anxiety can devastate examination performance. The purpose of this chapter is to present strategies for addressing examination-related anxiety.

## UNDERSTANDING THE CAUSES OF TEST ANXIETY

Anxiety is ultimately about failure and its consequences. An overly anxious person likely believes that failure is inevitable and the consequences are severe. To combat this mind-set, it is necessary to confront its causes. The two most common reasons for uncontrolled anxiety are (a) not knowing what to expect and (b) self-doubt about one's ability to effectively respond to an important challenge.

## Fear of the Unknown

Simply because something is mysterious, or new, or unknown does not guarantee that it will produce anxiety. For example, exploring a national forest or taking a tour in a new city are both experiences linked to something novel and perhaps mysterious, but they do not necessarily generate excess anxiety. To produce anxiety, the unknown must be linked with a sense of threat. Walking down a dark street in a crime-ridden neighborhood in an unfamiliar part of a strange city is likely to produce anxiety for most people. Being lost would only add to this. The difference between this experience and walking through a well-kept park is the possibility of danger.

To combat anxiety, it is necessary to address the unknown by acquiring information or experience and to respond to or prepare for any perceived threat or danger. In the context of the SLLA examination, danger is defined as failure. Removing the mystery of the examination is simply the act of acquiring information about its structure, requirements, and other aspects as described above. Of course, these two are linked. The more you learn about the SLLA, the less likely you are to be fearful because you do not know what to expect.

However, as you acquire information about the examination, if you learn that you are not prepared to do well, it is likely that your performance anxiety will increase. A systematic plan of preparation and study for the examination, as outlined above, provides an examinee with a means of addressing the dangers associated with it. In other words, knowing what to expect on the exam and acquiring experience with the examination is a necessary part of reducing anxiety about the experience and thus increasing the likelihood of maximum performance.

## Self-Doubt Causes Fear

If an examinee has doubt as to his/her ability to perform well on an examination, chances are that the person will not perform well. If these doubts are based on an objective assessment of the person's level of mastery of the content of the examination, then the solution is simple: study and increase content mastery. However, these doubts can also come from sources that are extraneous to actual mastery level but that can be just as devastating as an absence of content mastery. Below we offer a series of steps for identifying sources of doubt and addressing them.

### Step 1: Find Out What You Believe

To defeat the enemy, you must know the enemy. This idiom is certainly true when it comes to positive thinking relative to performance on an important examination. If an examinee doubts that he/she will perform well, this doubt must be grounded in something and have a source. A first step in confronting self-doubt is to identify its sources. Several typical sources of self-doubt are presented below. These, unfortunately, are often rehearsed mentally on an ongoing basis, and their effect is to lessen effort and dampen performance.

## Step 2: Gather Evidence to Contradict or Counter Negative Thinking

It is almost certainly the case that any negative belief is only partially based in reality. In fact, in many instances self-doubt is grounded in an unusual experience that has a heightened emotional charge, such as a team losing a championship game, even though their record for the season was otherwise spotless. Feelings of inadequacy associated with this one event may overshadow numerous examples of exceptional performance and lead to an overall sense of failure and self-doubt. To counter these feelings of inadequacy, it is necessary to get a balanced picture. In particular, identify and list the positive things that contradict or counter the negative experience. Several positive statements are offered for the negative self-statements listed in table 3.1. In each instance, the pattern is to collect personal experiences and evidence from others.

## Step 3: Devise a Plan to Acquire or Develop Additional Evidence to Counter the Negative

It is one thing to identify things you have done in the past that counter a negative belief about your potential. While this is helpful, it is also necessary to structure your experiences and actions in such a manner as to produce additional evidence of your competence. For example, if you find that you truly believe that you do not have firm mastery of measurement concepts, study these and self-administer examinations that show the ability to define key concepts and use them appropriately. These small successes are the building blocks for a new belief system. It is important to emphasize that the initial effort to confront a negative belief should be small, so as to ensure the likelihood of success. Larger steps come naturally.

## Step 4: Emphasize the Positive and Deny the Negative an Audience

As previously mentioned above, there is a tendency for many people to hold a negative self-image and to constantly rehash and rehearse negative self-statements. In fact, the very opposite is necessary. The positive must be emphasized, and every possible effort must be made to deny negative statements an audience. Below are some suggestions for emphasizing the positive and de-emphasizing the negative:

Table 3.1. Negative Self-Statements and Counterevidence

| Negative Statements about Self | Evidence to the Contrary |
|---|---|
| I don't know this stuff. | - Take a tally of what you do know.- List things you have read or studied.- Recall examples of when you demonstrated mastery.- Recall examples of occasions when others indicated that you have shown mastery. |
| I'm not smart. | - List examples of when you acted or responded in a way that showed intelligence or competence.- List intellectual accomplishments.- Recall examples of when others reported to you that you were intelligent. |
| I can't write. | - Find examples of things you have written well.- Identify things about your writing that you like and think are good.- Recall examples of things you have written that others thought were done well. |
| I'm too lazy to study. | - List examples of occasions on which you showed thrift or initiative.- Recall examples of occasions on which others thought you showed thrift or initiative. |
| I panic and freak out. | - Recall occasions on which you demonstrated calm and composure in the face of a challenging situation.- Recall instances in which others have indicated that you acted in a calm way in the face of a stressful situation. |
| I have no discipline. | - List instances in which you have showed discipline and purpose.- Recall instances in which others have indicated that you aced in a disciplined way. |

- Post evidence of your accomplishments in your space, in your office, on your desk, and in other places.
- Remind yourself frequently of the accomplishments that contradict negative self-statements.
- Stop negative thoughts as soon as you become aware of them. Counter the negative and shift your mental focus to something positive.
- Avoid horror stories and other comments that have the effect on you of raising anxiety levels or decreasing self-confidence about the exam.
- Avoid discussing the exam with people inclined to accept failure.
- Avoid discussing the exam with people who do not think you can handle it.

## *Step 5: Engage in Purposeful Mental Programming*

Shameless, blatant mental programming can be a useful tool for increasing overall productivity. The following steps are some ways of accomplishing this:

- Write down and repeat daily those things that you want to happen or need to believe about yourself in terms of ability to deal with the examination.
- Develop mental images of yourself accomplishing those things you want to happen, doing well on the exam, successfully studying material related to the exam, and so on.

## DEALING WITH ANXIETY

What do you do when before or during an exam you find yourself consumed with anxiety about an examination? Your body is rigid, you feel pain and panic, and your mind is a morass of emotions and thoughts. The answer is to (a) relax, (b) take an objective assessment of what is going on, and (c) focus on action and execute.

## Relax

An important point to emphasize when dealing with an anxiety attack is that you are most effective when you relax and act in a deliberate manner. If the mind, body, and emotions are in turmoil, little that is productive can happen. To address this, there are a number of relaxation techniques that others have found to be effective:

- Take slow, deep breaths and focus on your breathing. This helps to both focus the mind and generate a sense of calm.
- Tense and relax the muscles. Doing this helps relax the muscles and lessens the overall feeling of stress.
- Take a mental break. Focus momentarily on relaxing and calming thoughts. This is akin to fleeing a stress-producing situation long enough to regain composure.

## Take an Objective Assessment of What Is Happening

In the midst of an anxiety attack, ask yourself the following questions: Why am I panicking? What is going on? What can I do to get back to work? These, ideally, will start the process of rational self-assessment, from which a strategy of re-engagement can be formulated. If you know what caused the attack, you can focus on it and address it in a purposeful way.

For example, if your anxiety raced to unhealthy levels because you encountered a problem you could not answer, then consider moving on to one you can, answering it to the degree that you can, and then actually moving on, recalling what you have already accomplished on the exam. The point is that (a) you identify the cause of the elevated anxiety level, (b) make some assessment of the likely impact, and (c) determine a rational next course of action.

## Focus on Action

Moving from inaction caused by anxiety to purposeful action is an act of will. At some point in the process of reflecting on the causes and next steps, it will be necessary to simply act. Take the next step. Read the next prompt and write down some initial thoughts. The bottom line is that endless review and contemplation will not get the exam completed in a timely fashion, and a good understanding of this fact helps avoid slipping into procrastination.

As noted in previous chapters, technological advances have made the job of test preparation much easier. This is certainly true of anxiety and relaxation. The number of mobile apps focused on reducing stress, promoting meditation, and eliminating anxiety has grown exponentially. These may involve soothing music or other sounds, verbal coaching, and even games. An important part of an overall plan is to acquire apps that seem to help you achieve the level of calm that facilitates your study or focus.

## CONCLUSION

In this chapter, the causes and potential devastating impact of anxiety on test performance were discussed. The causes of anxiety were discussed, and a series of ways of addressing it were presented. It is important for the examinee to recognize that while some degree of anxiety can be a positive and motivating factor, too much can be an obstacle and should be addressed. The techniques discussed in this chapter can be considered as tools that are helpful.

*Chapter Four*

# Physical Preparation

A common misconception among many students is that a cram session improves performance. The conditions under which peak mental performance occur are well documented. They include the following: having a sufficient amount of rest, maintaining a healthful diet, and getting healthful levels of physical exercise.

## EXERCISE

Regular aerobic exercise promotes a sense of well-being, enhances mental functioning, and increases the stamina needed to handle stressful situations. Researchers have shown that exercise reduces stress and anxiety, enhances self-confidence and a sense of accomplishment, and may trigger chemical reactions in the brain that improve memory and concentration. The evidence is also that these benefits accrue from a regular aerobic pattern that is not overly strenuous, as might be associated with preparing for a marathon.

A regular, moderate aerobic exercise schedule may consist of daily walks, jogging, or spending twenty minutes a day on an air bike or treadmill at the local gym. The definition of moderate depends on one's level of fitness. Athletes may have a definition of moderate that most non-athletes would consider extreme and highly stressful. A useful gauge is to exercise at a rate at which you can carry on a conversation or hum a tune. As your level of fitness increases, it is likely that your performance level will also increase.

The benefits of exercise are believed to be linked to the increased blood flow and release of hormones and adrenaline that are stimulated during exercise. Blood flow increases to the brain and muscles, which stimulates brain activity and relieves the stress and strain muscles may experience as a result of stress or anxiety. The hormone adrenalin is also released during exercise and provides a boost of energy that can stimulate muscles and brain functions. Finally, exercise, particularly strenuous exercise, is related to the production of endorphins, which act to reduce pain and increase feelings of enjoyment and well-being.

## SLEEP AND REST

The evidence on the benefits of sleep is well known. The lack of sleep leads to a steady deterioration of mental functioning. Sleep deprivation studies have shown that a person who goes without sleep for an extended period of time behaves in ways symptomatic of alcohol intoxication: sluggish responses to stimuli, impaired short-term memory, inability to concentrate, and a host of other negative outcomes. Similarly, sleep deprivation impairs physiological processes and can lead to chronic fatigue, irritability, a reduced resistance to infections and other emotional and physiological consequences.

The evidence seems clear; a balanced approach to an examination includes regular sleep and rest. The exact amount of sleep needed to promote mental functioning varies with individuals but is typically between five and eight hours. Even more important, according to researchers, is the need of the body to get sufficient amounts of the right kinds of sleep. Sleep can be divided into five stages. The first four stages progress from light sleep, in which a person can be easily awakened, to stages 3 and 4, called deep sleep, in which the eyes and muscles stop moving and brain activity slows to a crawl.

Following deep sleep is the so-called rapid eye movement (REM) stage, in which dreams occur, muscles stiffen, eyes move rapidly, and the heart rate increases. It is this last stage that precedes waking. Too much or too little of the REM stage or the others can be detrimental to performance. Too much REM sleep, for example, has been linked to depression and other negative emotional states. Similarly, too little has been linked to a reduced capacity to perform complex cognitive tasks, decreases in alertness, and an overall lessened ability to perform mentally and physically. Researchers report that sleep disorders are common and that most go undiagnosed.

Sleep disorders are conditions that disrupt the normal sleep cycle and reduce the amount of quality sleep gotten by the body. They vary with respect to their seriousness, duration, and cause. According to researchers, most sleep disorders, especially mild forms, are common, and most go undiagnosed. One of the most common of these is a mild restriction of the upper airway. This can result from a sinus infection, allergies, medications, or some other condition that impedes an individual's ability to take in air during sleep. The result is that the people wake often, reducing the amount of deep or REM sleep and increasing the amount of time in the light sleep stage.

While increases in light sleep have no appreciable impact on mental functioning, decreases in deep sleep or REM sleep can significantly impair both mental and physical functioning. Fortunately, most mild restrictions to the upper airway are of short duration and can be treated with over-the-counter prescriptions or devices such as those designed to reduce snoring, a common symptom of upper airway obstruction.

A more serious sleep disorder linked to upper airway obstruction is sleep apnea. Sleep apnea is a disorder of breathing during the night. It is typically associated with loud snoring and results from the fact that an individual is struggling to get sufficient amounts of oxygen during sleep. The symptoms of sleep apnea include frequent waking during the night, waking up in the morning without a feeling of renewal, feelings of fatigue during the day, difficulty staying alert or awake during the day, or waking up with a head-ache.

The good news is that sleep apnea can be treated. There are many devices which help keep the upper airway open so that it is easier to breathe during the night. Many of the over-the-counter devices designed to reduce or elimi-nate snoring can help someone affected with sleep apnea. Some other life-style changes include losing weight, reducing alcohol consumption, and sleeping on one's side. However, sleep apnea can be a serious condition, and if you suspect that you are affected, you should discuss it with your doctor.

It is also important to note that while snoring is typically associated with sleep apnea, everyone who snores is not necessarily suffering from this con-dition. Snorers who experience the conditions mentioned above, or who have periods of quiet followed by gasps for breath, or who snore so loudly as to disturb others may be suffering from a form of sleep apnea and should discuss their condition with a physician.

Insomnia is a common term associated with a sleep dysfunction. Insom-nia is a sleeping disorder in which an individual (a) has difficulty falling asleep, (b) has difficulty staying asleep, or (c) wakes before the sleep cycle is completed. Insomnia can be caused by a deeper underlying sleep disorder such as apnea; it can be caused by excessive consumption of caffeine and other stimulants, physical pain, stress, and other intense emotional feelings. Insomnia is the result of an underlying condition, and identifying that condi-tion is the first step in combating insomnia.

Insomnia can be of short duration, as that resulting from a stressful event, or be a longterm, chronic condition. As with any sleep-related problem, it can lead to impaired cognitive functioning, negative emotional states, and slug-gishness. If you feel you suffer from chronic insomnia, try some of the sleep-promoting techniques discussed below, but the condition can be the result of a problem requiring medical attention and should be discussed with your physician.

## Strategies for Maintaining a Healthful Sleep Pattern

There are several techniques that have been shown to help promote a healthful sleep pattern. The following suggestions, albeit not comprehensive, include many of the more frequently offered recommendations.

*Maintain a consistent sleep schedule.* Go to sleep at specific times and for a consistent amount of time. Delaying the time at which you go to sleep or wake can disrupt the sleep cycle and reduce the amount of deep or REM sleep you obtain.

*Avoid sleeping in an environment in which you are likely to be awakened frequently.* Frequent interruptions to sleep tend to lead to less of the deep or REM sleep the body needs. Intermittent noises as those that come from televisions, phone conversations, and other disruptions can make it impossible to achieve deep sleep. Places susceptible to these disruptions are to be avoided, and if that is not possible, ear plugs and other noise reduction techniques should be used to eliminate or reduce the incidence of disruptions.

*Avoid bright lights during sleep.* Bright lights act as stimulants and trigger an awakened state in the body. Darkened rooms have been shown to be most conducive to sleep. Should this not be possible, eye patches can help promote a healthful sleep cycle.

*Keep room temperatures comfortable.* If the body is unusually cold or hot, it is difficult for most people to achieve deep sleep or the REM stage. Careful sleep planning should include consideration of the room temperature necessary for an individual to be comfortable.

*Avoid smoking or consuming large amounts of alcohol or caffeine before your normal bedtime.* Caffeine is a stimulant and can make it difficult to achieve the relaxed state that will lead to sleep. Alcohol and cigarettes can act to restrict airflow and lead to frequent awakening during the night. All can reduce the amount you get of quality sleep that the body needs.

*Avoid creating an expectation that you will have difficulty sleeping.* It is not uncommon for people to develop an attitude that they will have difficulty sleeping. In most cases, this may be linked to some major event such as a wedding or long trip. Since these are usually specific to an event, they will not likely be of an extended duration. This is fortunate because the expectation that one will have difficulty sleeping is almost always realized. Individuals who believe that they will have trouble sleeping usually do. The solution is to avoid this expectation.

*Avoid excessive napping during daytime hours.* Some napping during the course of the day can enhance mental performance, such as a quick nap after a large lunch. However, prolonged napping during the day can reduce the amount of deep or REM sleep achieved during the night. Deep sleep and REM sleep are most likely to occur at night as the body cools and mental activity decreases. Extended daytime naps have the potential to reduce the amount of time people spend sleeping during maximum sleep periods. Most daytime napping is closer to light sleep than either of the other two.

*Moderate exercise can promote sleep.* Research evidence shows that there is a relation between exercise and the amount of time spent in deep sleep. Daily exercise of moderate intensity promotes longer periods of deep sleep.

## DIET

There is growing evidence that mental performance is intimately linked to diet. The brain is a complex organism, but researchers are learning that certain foods are key to the chemical reactions in the brain that facilitate memory, reasoning, concentration, and a host of other cognitive functions.

*Do not skip breakfast.* A consistent recommendation from nutritionists is that breakfast is an important meal. There is evidence that people who skip breakfast function less well cognitively throughout the day than those who do not. A breakfast high in carbohydrates (whole grain cereals, fruits, etc.) increases the glucose level in the blood, which increases the energy supply to the brain.

*Eat foods close to their form in nature.* The processes used to convert foods to what we usually see on our supermarket shelves often destroys many of the nutrients put there by nature and can create an imbalance that makes it difficult for the body to use the nutrients that are present. The solution is to eat foods as close to their natural state as possible.

*Increase intake of grains, beans, and legumes.* These foods supply many nutrients the brain can use and promote the chemical processes that occur.

*Antioxidants.* Antioxidants inhibit many of the negative effects of the oxidation of oxygen in the body. This process can lead to significant damage to tissue, especially brain cells. Blueberries and foods high in vitamin C (e.g., orange juice) are antioxidants, which help prevent damage to brain cells.

*B vitamins.* B vitamins promote the breakdown of carbohydrates into energy for the brain and the breakdown of fats and proteins for the nervous system. They are widely recognized for their important role in brain functioning. Foods high in B vitamins include eggs, rice, whole grain cereals, fruits, nuts, red meats, cheese, fish, and so on.

*Choline.* Recent research shows that choline plays a key role in learning, memory, and overall brain functioning. Foods high in choline include eggs, red meats, milk, and so on.

*Omega-3 fatty acids.* Omega-3 fatty acids are essential for a number of brain functions. They are mainly found in fish, leading many to label fish as a "brain" food.

*Iodine.* Iodine has been linked to decision making, initiative, and a host of other brain functions. Iodinated foods include salt, meats, and so on.

*Caffeine.* There is evidence that caffeine is a stimulant for mental functioning.

*Water.* Levels of hydration are widely accepted as being a factor in brain functioning.


## CONCLUSION


Having a sufficient amount of rest, maintaining a healthful diet, and getting healthful levels of physical exercise are all critical components for being physically prepared to take examinations. Most standardized tests/examinations are time intensive. In the case of the SLLA, test takers must be focused for four hours. Therefore, physical preparation is definitely an added advantage.

This chapter is the last in part I of this book. The remainder of the book focuses on the specifics of the SLLA.

*Chapter Five*

# NCLB (Where Are We Now?)

In the first edition of *Passing the Leadership Test*, we cited Graham[1] (1991). He suggested twenty years ago that it was no longer viable to allow children to "slide through" academically weak curricula. The staggering achievement of American students was an emerging area of concern for educators and policy makers in the 1990s. For decades, the national focus on student achievement has been linked to national initiatives and goals with funding in education aligned to national goals. As evidenced in the 1950s and 1960s, the launching of Sputnik by Russia was followed by great emphases on mathematics and science in the United States, with funding shifting and supporting these areas.

More and more attention has shifted to the performance of K–12 students. In Fullan's[2] (2010) *All Systems Go*, Senge notes the declining performance of American students. Although there are great schools and great districts in the United States, there are wide disparities in student performance. Furthermore, the overall performance is alarming. A half century ago (1960s,) the nation was among the top world ranking in education based on high-school qualifications. The current ranking is in the bottom half of advanced countries; and the rate in which the decline has occurred also appears rather rapid. In 1995, the United States was rated first in postsecondary graduation rates. By 2005, the ranking was fourteenth.

In March 2010, Secretary of Education Arnie Duncan released the reauthorization of the Elementary and Secondary Education Act.[3] The 2010 reauthorization increases expectations and rigor from foundations established in the 2001 No Child Left Behind Act. Teacher and school leader accountability are emerging challenges of the heightened awareness. Lovell (2003) suggested that when a student has an ineffective teacher for two consecutive years, this is a barrier that a student will more than likely not overcome.[4]

Information released from the Southern Region Education Board[5] (SREB) validates the importance of the role of the school leader. According to SREB, the school leader can impact as much as 20 percent of the achievement in schools. Frank Siccone[6] (2012) suggests that the leader can impact as much as 25 percent of the achievement in the building.

Obviously, the heightened focus on the roles of teachers and school leaders in student achievement has led to much discussion on what the characteristics and attributes of an effective school leader are and what the effective characteristics and attributes of an effective teacher are. Todd Whitaker[7] (2004) says that an effective teacher is an effective leader, and an effective leader is an effective teacher. Teachers that are "great" have leadership skills, and "great" leaders are effective teachers.

In this volume, much of the focus is on the role of effective leaders, standards for school leaders, and the School Leader Licensure Assessment. In the remainder of this chapter, accountability and its implications are discussed further. In chapter 6, the standards for school leadership (Educational Leadership Constituent Council [ELCC] and Interstate School Leaders Licensure Consortium [ISLLC]) are the areas of concentration. In chapter 7, the standards as linked to the examination are highlighted. And in chapter 8, practical case studies as linked to the standards are presented.

One of the important roles of an effective leader is building leadership capacity among teachers. This concept of building leadership capacity is embedded in standard 2 of ISLLC and ELCC and is a facet of instructional leadership. The concept of instructional leadership is the focus of standard 2 of both ISLLC and ELLC. The school leader as an instructional leader provides leadership pertinent to effective classroom instruction. Setting high expectations for teaching and learning along with building effective school cultures are among the critical concepts for instructional leadership.

Multiple perspectives and several models of instructional leadership are highlighted in *The Relevance of Instructional Leadership*[8] (2011). The shift in the role of the principal to instructional leadership is emphasized. What was required for a principal to be effective twenty years ago is very different in this era of accountability. In addition, the importance of school culture as aligned with instructional leadership is cited in *The Relevance of Instructional Leadership*. Pertinent leadership skills and traits are essential in the role of the leader in facilitating positivism in the cultures and climates of schools. Lashway's perspective of developing instructional leadership is also discussed.[9] Further detail on instructional leadership is provided in chapter 6.

There are different perspectives on what constitutes effective leaders and effective teachers and on what the more critical variables to student achievement are. In spite of the differences in perspectives, we believe that most educators will agree that effective teaching and effective leadership are critical to student achievement and that there is an interrelationship between effective teaching and effective leadership as Whitaker suggests. It appears that accountability for school leaders and teachers is constantly intensifying.

## ACCOUNTABILITY AND ITS IMPLICATIONS

Accountability and standardized testing in educational entities are generally mentioned in the same sentence because standardized testing is one of the major measures of accountability. For decades, students in K–12 schools have been required to take, and in many instances score mastery on, standardized tests. The rapid growth of the use of standardized tests in schools expanded in the middle of the twentieth century. In the 1960s, the federal government embraced the use of standardized tests to measure the success of schools receiving Title I funds.

Title I was funded by the Elementary and Secondary Education Act. Colleges and universities began using standardized tests as well after World War II. The standardized testing era of the 1960s initiated criticism. The criticism led to the implementation of criterion reference and minimum competency testing.[10]

The wave of testing in higher education began as a result of reform efforts. According to Henniger (2004),[11] the results of the reform efforts of the 1980s initiated changes in higher standards for students in K–12 schools as well as additional rigor in teacher certification programs. Mandatory standardized testing was implemented in nearly every state. The two issues of higher standards for teachers and additional rigor for teachers are highly correlated. To expect more of students requires a higher level of professionalism from teachers.

In an effort to raise standards for students, the 1990s saw an influx in the use of high-stakes testing in K–12 schools.[12] The emphasis of testing in the 1990s shifted to open-ended items, performances, and tasks that supported critical thinking. According to Kennedy (2003),[13] the education community felt that multiple-choice items did not align with student learning and thinking.

The importance of standardized tests in public schools is being re-emphasized with a present link to standards. This renewed emphasis is supported by the NCLB legislation and reauthorization of the Elementary and Secondary Education Act. Since 2005–2006, students enrolled in grades three through eight in all schools in the nation were required to take standardized tests in reading and mathematics.[14] In the 2006–2007 academic school year, students were expected to take a science test as well.

Schools will constantly be evaluated based on the performance of students on standardized tests, and schools will be expected to demonstrate adequate yearly progress (AYP) in all major socioeconomic groups, ethnic groups, English-as-a-second-language learners, and special education students.[15] According to Peterson (2005),[16] the long-term goal of NCLB is to have all students pass with proficiency in reading and mathematics by the 2013–2014 school year. And it is important to note that Zigmond and Kloo (2008)[17] argue that students with disabilities cannot be omitted from accountability systems, and the performances of students with disabilities must be reported in statewide assessments both with others and in disaggregated groups.

As previously alluded to, the NCLB legislation and the 2010 reauthorization also have implications for classroom teachers. In addition to being evaluated on the basis of the performance of their students on standardized tests, NCLB mandates that every classroom has a "highly qualified teacher." Highly qualified refers to the possession of a college degree and full teacher certification in addition to evidence of teacher–subject matter knowledge. States have the autonomy to add additional requirements to the federal definition of "highly qualified."[18] Teacher certification programs have targeted four areas in an effort to raise standards—testing requirements, curriculum requirements, introduction of field experiences earlier, and continuing requirements after graduation.

According to Henniger (2000),[19] many states are requiring aspiring teachers to pass licensure teaching tests prior to graduation from a teaching program. State boards of education also continue to raise minimum scores, and some states have bolstered new assessments. Furthermore, many states have eliminated lifetime certification. Teachers are being required to engage in professional development, which can lead to even further standardized testing. The challenge to raise teacher standards is directly linked to recruiting and retaining qualified individuals into the teacher preparation programs and profession.

Both of these issues are complicated by the projected teacher shortage. According to the National Education Association, two million teachers will be needed in the next decade. Forty-two states have issued temporary licensure as a means to fill vacancies.[20] It is noteworthy that the national economic trends have negatively impacted the number of employable teachers in some areas of the nation.

The additional layer that has been added to accountability for teachers and university departments of teacher education is the value-added model. In Louisiana, the Act 54 legislation is linked to the value-added model. Beginning in 2012–2013, 50 percent of the evaluations of teachers will be based on the learning of students as measured by the model (www.doe.state.la.us). The value-added model was developed by Dr. William Sanders, who worked in the field of agricultural genetics at the University of Tennessee. In the 1980s, Sanders and a team of researchers developed a model to determine teacher effectiveness as linked to standardized testing. The initial model received very little attention and was and is still very controversial; however, the value-added model is becoming more widely used. [21]

According to the Louisiana Department of Education's web link (www.doe.state.la.us), value-added is a statistical model that combines the test data of students and demographical factors to determine whether the students made more or less academic progress than anticipated. It is a fairer way to examine results based on the progress made by students. For teachers, value-added evaluates changes in the student achievement of students across an academic year. Teachers are rated (general ratings include below average, average, above average) on the performances of students.

As cited previously, valued-added is very controversial. However, The Center for Greater Philadelphia cites the following as advantages of value-added as linked to improving the requirements of AYP:

- It tracks individual students over time. NCLB's Adequate Yearly Progress requirements don't follow the same student from, say, fourth grade to fifth grade; rather, they compare this year's fourth graders with last year's fourth graders, whether or not the new cohort resembles the one from the previous year. In short, AYP can amount to an apples-to-oranges comparison. It cannot show the progress made by particular students or groups of students over time which is the only way to make valid comparisons of students' performance.
- It encourages schools to raise the achievement of all students, not just the subset of students whose improvement will satisfy AYP goals.
- It focuses attention on individual classrooms. Under NCLB, schools—rather than teachers and administrators—are held directly accountable for student achievement, and there are no rewards for success, only sanctions for failure. However, while struggling students are indeed found in classrooms of all types, data from Tennessee make unequivocally clear that they are not randomly distributed: they are found disproportionately in classrooms with ineffective instruction. If the focus is on struggling students rather than on the teachers who are providing ineffective instruction, scarce resources will be devoted to the symptoms rather than their underlying causes. When used at the classroom level, value-added assessment gives individual teachers and administrators specific data describing two key patterns—the focus and impact—of their instruction, allowing them to target interventions where they are needed.
- It is a better measure of school improvement. Under NCLB, school progress is an all-or-nothing affair—either the school makes AYP or it does not. However, value-added assessment shows any amount of progress that a school has made, even if it falls short of the AYP threshold. It does not sugarcoat low-achievement, but it does acknowledge the actual steps—both small and large—that schools make. [22]

For departments of teacher education, the departments are rated on the basis of the performances of the K–12 students for teacher education candidates (graduates of the colleges). The ratings are usually provided by core areas— English language arts, mathematics, science, and social studies. In order to receive scores, a sufficient number of graduates must be available for each individual core area. The challenge often comes in providing a rating to programs with low completion rates.

The pressures for schools to produce highly educated and versatile students are perhaps greater now than ever before. Old practices, philosophies, and polices have been challenged. Thompson (2003) notes eight characteristics necessary for schools to be high performing—standards-based, clear mission, school climate, assessment, professional development, focused use of resources, data collection, and communication.[23] Blankstein (2010)[24] suggests that effective schools are the result of effective learning communities, and he has embedded in his work the work of several authors along with ISLLC. The factors suggested by Blankstein are: common mission, vision, values and goals; achievement focus for all students with systems of prevention and intervention; collaboration focus on teaching and learning; data use to guide decision making and continuous improvement; active engagement from family and community; and building sustainable leadership capacity.

Murphy (1999)[25] acknowledges the vigorous work in most states to set academic standards for approximately fifty-two million K–12 students and devise ways to measure the standards. He also recognizes the rigorous standards for approximately three million teachers. However, Murphy (1999)[26] suggests that the effort to raise standards for teachers and students will "fall short" if states and school districts do not set standards for school leaders. The challenge for raising standards for school leaders is complicated by an anticipated shortage of talented candidates. It is anticipated that the number of administrative positions will increase by 20 percent in the next few years.

Seyfarth (2005) suggests that the pool of prospective administrators is shrinking. Fewer teachers apply to fill principal vacancies.[27] Cusic (2003) cites the findings of school superintendents—60 percent of superintendents surveyed suggest that their districts face shortages of qualified applicants. Individuals outside of the districts are filling positions that were traditionally filled with staff from within the districts.[28] According to NGA (2003),[29] the findings of research also suggest that current and aspiring principals lack the essential skills for leadership roles in our nation's schools. A recent study conducted by Public Agenda revealed that 29 percent of superintendents believe that the quality of principals is declining.[30]

# A BLUEPRINT FOR REFORM: REAUTHORIZATION OF THE ELEMENTARY AND SECONDARY ACT

As previously cited, the reauthorization adds rigor to *NCLB*. The four areas addressed in the reauthorization are: (1) improving teacher and principal effectiveness to ensure that every classroom has a great teacher and every school has a great leader; (2) providing information to families to help them evaluate and improve their children's schools and to educators to help them improve their students' learning; (3) implementing college- and career-ready standards and developing improved assessments aligned with those standards; and (4) improving student learning and achievement in the nation's lowest-performing schools by providing intensive support and effective interventions. [31]

In addition to the four areas addressed, there are key priorities that the federal government has established. Those areas are college- and career-ready students; great teachers and leaders in every school; equity and opportunity for all students; excellence and raising the bar; and innovation and continuous improvement. There are many details in each of these areas; however, an overview of major concepts will be provided. Raising standards for students, improving assessments, and improving completion rates in education are the goals aligned with college and career readiness.

States are encouraged to adopt standards in English language arts and mathematics centered on college and career readiness with better assessments. Forty-four states have adopted common core assessments, and some of the states are in the process of developing assessments. Partnership for Assessment of Readiness for College and Careers (PARCC) is the consortium that is currently in the process of drafting the assessments. PARCC is composed of educators who are K–12 leaders and employees of higher-education entities. [32]

The administration of the assessment will take place in 2014–2015 with field testing starting in 2012–2013. The goal of the PARCC college-ready assessments is to prepare students to enter with greater preparation levels for completion of degrees and certificate programs. Several studies have been conducted using different methodologies to access completion rates of students in four years of college. According to information provided by the government's web link, the current rate at which college students complete degree programs in four years is below 50 percent in most, if not all, instances. [33] When we couple the dropout rate from high school with the four-year completion rates from universities, these are startling facts that need to improve.

The intended advantages of the design of the assessment system are increased meaning of standards, higher-quality tests, maximized used of technology, and improved capabilities of cross-state comparability. In addition, the intended outcomes are that achievement results will be reported using a clear definition of college and career readiness, results will be compared against a common high standard of readiness, accountability policies should be better in helping with improvement, and instruction should be improved in multiple ways.[34]

According to the web link www.corestandards.org, the initiative for the common core standards is state led by the Council of Chief State School Officers (CCSSO) and the National Governors Association Center for Best Practices (NGA Center). CCSSO also led the redesign of the revised ISLCC standards for 2008. One of the goals in the development of the standards is to provide teachers with consistent and appropriate benchmarks identifying the knowledge and skills students should have within their K–12 education.

Key concepts of the standards include that they are aligned with college and work expectations, are clear, understandable, and consistent, include rigorous content and application of knowledge through higher order skills, build upon strengths and lessons of current state standards, are informed by other top-performing countries so that all students are prepared to succeed in our global economy, and are evidence based.[35]

The principle of great teachers and leaders in every school centers on promoting effective teachers and principals, placement of teachers and leaders in areas where they are most needed, and strengthening teacher and leadership preparation and recruitment. The components of teacher preparation and leadership preparation and recruitment were emphasized in previous reform efforts. Previously in the chapter, challenges and additional rigor added to teacher education programs were cited. Many states or other entities are focusing on long-term professional development for teachers. There is a focus on rewarding excellence in professionals as aligned with the placement of great teachers and principals in schools. Obviously, high-quality leadership and teaching are supported by meaningful and relevant professional development.

The key priority of equity and opportunity for all students is a challenge that has evolved historically. Many federal and state legislations address funding to improve equity in educational opportunities for specific populations. Kozol pointed out in two publications, *Savage Inequalities*[36] and *The Shame of the Nation: The Restoration of Apartheid Schooling in America*[37], the range of differences in funding schools that occurs across states, within states, and often within districts. He suggests that these are inequities. In a summary of articles on funding schools in the 1990s, district representatives with a surplus in funding suggested that funding is not a significant variable as it relates to student achievement and the operation of districts. Districts lacking funding suggest that funding is significant.

Meeting the needs of diverse and/or specific students is perhaps more critical for K–12 schools in this era as linked to accountability. School districts must demonstrate that special-needs students, at-risk students, English-language learners, and minority groups demonstrate comparable levels of growth on achievement as compared to the majority population. Support for homeless students, migrant students, rural students, and neglected students is included in the legislation.

The 2010 legislation also calls for drastic changes in lowest-performing schools that continuously underperform. The encouragement to work toward/on reform is provided through incentives like "Race to the Top." Comprehensive school reform is the goal of raising the bar. Several theorists have suggested that past reform efforts have been unsuccessful because many reform efforts have been fragmented and piecemeal. Fullan was cited in the introduction to chapter 5. He points out that the rapid decline in achievement occurred simultaneously with a costly reform agenda and suggests that the real problem in school reform can be the "one-size-fits-all fixes." The final priority of the reauthorization is to promote continuous improvement. Supporting sustainability of improvement becomes the monumental challenge for educators and policy makers.

Blankstein[38] (2010) discusses critical components of sustainability for K–12 school leadership in his publication *Failure Is Not an Option*. He says that sustainability is much more than endurance; it is also "more than life and death of change." Blankstein adapts the perspective of Hargreaves and Fink (2005).[39] From their perspective, "Sustainable educational leadership and improvement preserves and develops deep learning for all that spreads and lasts, in ways that do no harm to indeed create positive benefits for others around us, now and into the future."[40] Obviously, the role of the school leader is critical in K–12 schools.

There are ten practical notions that guide sustainability in schools; they include

- refocus the curriculum;
- begin discussions about achievement and how to raise it with the conversation and reflection about learning that underpins the achievement;
- include leadership succession plans in all school improvement plans;
- make learning team membership a condition of employment for all teachers;
- consider the legacy desired to leave as a leader;
- establish collaborative relationships with schools and entities in communities;

- provide coaching and professional development for teachers and staff; and
- develop genuine interests in schools and districts—one way is through classroom observations. [41]

The importance of sustainability of achievement is therefore supported by courageous leadership and professional learning communities. Leaders in K–12 schools and district leaders must begin with a core that creates organizational meaning. That meaning should provide the parameters for clarity of purpose. When the purpose is established in an organization (specifically for schools), it is supported by meaningful data.

## AMERICA'S STORY: A NATION AT RISK

Our current reform agenda is obviously NCLB and the reauthorization of the Elementary and Secondary Education Act. NCLB initiated in the office of President George W. Bush in 2001. The major emphases of NCLB were

- improving achievement of the disadvantaged;
- recruitment and training of teachers and principals;
- language instruction for limited-English-proficient students;
- funding for federally impacted areas;
- reading first and literacy programs; and
- dropout prevention (NCLB, 2008). [42]

Interestingly, similar assertions were made nearly twenty years before. Improving the performance of students and educators was the major emphasis of *A Nation at Risk*. In the 1983 report, serious problems in American schools were identified. The problems included the military reports of significant funding on remediation for students leaving high schools; an increase in remedial mathematics courses offered at four-year institutions; lower achievement of students graduating from college; and a steady decline in science achievement. According to the National Commission on Excellence in Education [43] (1983), these problems were directly aligned with poor teaching, low expectations in classrooms, and a need to attract better teachers.

There are obvious concepts cited identically in both legislations (NCLB and *A Nation at Risk*)—recruitment and training of teachers, dropout prevention, and a need for specific curricular improvement. The obvious focus in NCLB and *A Nation at Risk* has direct implications for the classrooms and teachers. In 1983, the *Nation at Risk* task force recommended that teacher preparation programs be strengthened and academic programs be intensified. As previously cited, Henniger (2004) attributed *A Nation at Risk* to providing changes in two areas: higher standards for students and more demanding teacher certification programs. Clearly, to expect more of students requires that teachers "raise the bar" for themselves as well as "raise the bar" for students.

The core curriculum was proposed by Bonnet shortly after *A Nation at Risk*[44] . It consisted of four years of English, two years of foreign language, and three years of mathematics, science, and social studies. Many states have made additions, and some states currently use the core as a guiding parameter. The NCLB legislation shifted the focus for the nation to performance of students on standardized tests; some educational theorists might argue that the focus on standardized testing is a reshifting from a previous era. The requirements for student performance on standardized tests were previously discussed.

I think that all or most educators will agree that school reform is essential, or at least that improving the performance of the nation's students is critical. As previously addressed, Fullan[45] acknowledges that in some instances, there are good schools and students who are performing well, and that reform or change is possible. However, he suggests that many of the good schools are isolated, and it is our opinion that many of the "good things" occur in isolation. The change begins with the belief and vested interests from many stakeholders.

Peter Senge and colleagues (2008)[46] in *The Dance of Change* discuss the complexities of change. Senge along with his colleagues suggests that most significant change initiatives fail. They suggest that real change requires shifts in the way of thinking. This requires leaders to understand mechanisms that aid growth, means of catalyzing growth, factors that impede progress, and strategies to address the factors that impede growth. Senge (2008) and colleagues suggest that patience and urgency are required.

The real challenge for reform and improving performances of students is in schools where there is underperformance. The current accountability movements generally measure student performance by standardized testing, and the use of and/or focus on standardized testing is debated. There are proponents of testing who suggest that it will lead to improved performance of teachers and ultimately improved student performances. And the opponents suggest that education becomes a low priority when testing becoming the focus.

## CONCLUSION

Regardless of an embraced position and perspective on standardized testing, all or most educators will agree that change is needed in American schools. Change in American schools must be aligned with sustainable reform. The previously cited statistics validate the need for positive change. However, Blankstein (2010) suggests that the human dimension of change (the how and why of school reform) has to be clearly addressed. Without addressing this dimension, Blankstein suggests that we will continue to have disappointing results (2010.)[47]

## NOTES

1. Graham, P. (1991, November). What America Has Expected of Its Schools over the Past Century. Paper presented at the Conference on Democracy and Education, Chicago, Illinois.
2. Fullan, M. (2010). *All Systems Go: The Change Imperative for Whole System Reform*. California: Corwin.
3. A Blueprint for Reform, available at www2.ed.gov/policy/elsec/leg/blueprint/blueprint.pdf.
4. Lovell (2003),
5. SREB
6. Siccone, F. (2012). *Essential Skills for Effective School Leadership*. Boston: Pearson.
7. Whitaker, T. (2009). *What Great Teachers Do Differently*. New York: Eye on Education.
8. Jones, L. (2011). *The Relevance of Instructional Leadership*. California: Cognella.
9. Lashway
10. Kennedy, E. (2003). *Raising Test Scores for All Students*. California: Corwin.
11. Henniger, M. L. (2004). *The Teaching Experience: An Introduction to Reflective Practice*. Ohio: Pearson/Merrill/Prentice Hall.
12. Kennedy, E. (2003). *Raising Test Scores for All Students*. California: Corwin.
13. Ibid.
14. Bracey, G. (2003). The 13th Bracey Report on the Condition of Public Education. *Phi Delta Kappan* (85)2: 148–64.
15. Ibid.
16. Peterson, K. (2005). NCLB Goals and Penalties. Retrieved August 1, 2011, from www.stateline.org/live/ViewPage.action?siteNodeId=136&languageId=l&contentId=41611.
17. Zigmond, N., & Kloo, A. (2009). The Two Percent Student: Consideration and Consequences of Eligible Decisions. *Peabody Journal of Education* 84: 478–95.
18. Walsh, K. (2003, June 4). A Blessing in Disguise. *Education Week*, 28, 30.
19. Henniger, M. L. (2004). *The Teaching Experience: An Introduction to Reflective Practice*. Ohio: Pearson/Merrill/Prentice Hall.
20. Attracting and Keeping Quality Teachers. (2004, June). Retrieved from www.nea.org/teachershortage.
21. Center for Greater Philadelphia; Value-Added Assessment. Retrieved from www.cgp.upenn.edu/ope_value.html#8.
22. Ibid.
23. Thompson, S. (2003). A High-Performance School System. In F. M. Duffy, ed., *Courage, Passion, and Vision* (101–12).Lanham, MD: Scarecrow.
24. Blankstein, A. (2010). *Failure Is Not an Option*. California: Corwin.

25. Murphy, J. (1999, October). Putting New School Leaders to the Test. Retrieved from http://soe.csusb.edu/awaner/sleader.htm.

26. Ibid.

27. Seyfarth, J. (2005). *Human Resources Management to Effective School.* Boston: Pearson.

28. Cusic, K. (2003, May). The Principalship? No. Thanks. *Education Week,* 34, 44.

29. Mazzeo, C. (2003). Improving Teaching and Learning by Improving School Leadership. Issue Brief. NGA Center for Best Practices.

30. Ibid.

31. A Blueprint for Reform (The Reauthorization of the Elementary and Secondary Act). Retrieved from www2.ed.gov/policy/elsec/leg/blueprint/blueprint.pdf.

32. Ibid.

33. Changes in College Completion Rates, www2.ed.gov/pubs/CollegeForAll/completion.html.

34. Louisiana Department of Education, www.doe.state.la.us.

35. Common Core State Standards Initiative, www.corestandards.org.

36. Kozol, J. (1991). *Savage Inequalities: Children in America's Schools.* New York: Harper Perennial.

37. Kozol, J. (2005). *The Shame of the Nation: The Restoration of Apartheid Schooling in America.* New York: Three Rivers Press.

38. Blankstein, A. (2010). *Failure Is Not an Option.* California: Corwin.

39. Hargreaves, A., & Fink, D. (2005). *Sustainable Leadership.* San Francisco: Jossey-Bass.

40. Blankstein, A. (2006). *Failure Is Not an Option.* California: Corwin.

41. Ibid.

42. NCLB (2002). Retrieved from www.ed.gov/legilsation/ESEA02/.

43. National Commission on Excellence in Education. (1983). *A Nation at Risk: The Imperative for Educational Reform.* Washington, DC: U.S. Department of Education.

44. Springfield, S., Winfield, L., Milsap, M., Puma, M., Gamse, B., & Randall, B. (1994). *Urban and Suburban Rural Special Strategies for Educating Disadvantaged Children: First Year Report.* Baltimore: Johns Hopkins University. ERIC Document Reproduction Service No. ED 369854.

45. Fullan, M. (2010). *All Systems Go: The Change Imperative for Whole System Reform.* California: Corwin.

46. Senge, P., Kleiner, A. R., Roberts, C. H., Ross, R., Roth, G., & Smith, B. (2008). *The Dance of Change: The Challenges of Sustaining Momentum in Learning Organizations.* New York: Doubleday.

47. Blankstein, A. (2010). *Failure Is Not an Option.* California: Corwin.

*Chapter Six*

# ISLLC Standards and ELCC Standards

## THE COMMONALITIES

Anthes (2005) suggests that it is standards that put in place the "good starting point" for defining high-quality leaders. There have been several sets of leadership standards created over the years across multiple entities; however, one of the first sets of standards created were ISLLC. The Council of Chief State School Officers combined with a panel of educational experts to produce the first set of standards, composed of standards, dispositions, and performances for school leaders to meet.

In 2008, ISLLC restructured its standards. Anthes (2005) identified several additional entities that have established leadership standards and/or completed research on leadership practices. The National Association of Elementary School Principals (NAESP) and the Educational Leadership Constituent Council (ELCC) are among the entities that developed standards. Substantial work in the area of leadership has been completed by the Southern Regional Education Board (SREB) and McREL.

Anthes (2005) found that all standards generally align to the following categories:

- developing and articulating a vision;
- strategic decision making and implementation;
- promoting community engagement;
- creating a culture of learning;
- using data appropriately;
- understanding curriculum and instruction;
- seeking engagement from all staff;
- understanding effective management;

- providing high-quality professional growth opportunities to staff; and
- communicating effectively and honestly with staff, students, and community members.


## ISLLC


According to the article *About ISLLC*,[1] the ISLLC standards are based on

- a thorough analysis of what is known about effective educational leadership at the school levels;
- a comprehensive examination of the best thinking about the types of leadership for tomorrow's schools;
- syntheses of the thoughtful work on administrator standards developed by various national organizations, professional associations, and reform commissions; and
- in-depth discussions of leadership and administrative standards by leaders within each of the entities involved in the ISLLC.

Each of the standards begins with the same phrase—"A school administrator is an educational leader who promotes the success of all students by. . . ."[2] The following is the remaining of the text for the standards:

> Standard 1 (The Vision of Learning) facilitating the development, articulation, implementation, and stewardship of a vision of learning that is shared and supported by the school community,
>
> Standard 2 (The Culture of Teaching and Learning) advocating, nurturing, and sustaining a school culture and instructional program conducive to student learning and staff professional growth,
>
> Standard 3 (Management of Learning) ensuring management of the organization, operations, and resources for a safe, efficient, and effective learning environment,
>
> Standard 4 (Relations with Broader Community to Foster Learning) collaborating with families and community members, responding to diverse community interests and needs, and mobilizing community resources,
>
> Standard 5 (Integrity, Fairness, and Ethics in Learning) acting with integrity, with fairness, and in an ethical manner,
>
> Standard 6 (The Political, Social, Economic, Legal, and Cultural Context of Learning) understanding, responding to, and influencing the larger political, social, economic, legal, and cultural contexts.

# EDUCATIONAL LEADERSHIP CONSTITUENT COUNCIL (ELCC)

The ELCC standards are an extension of the ISLCC standards. The American Association for School Administrators (AASA), American Association for Supervision and Curriculum Development (AACD), National Association for Secondary School Principals (NASSP), and National Association for Elementary School Principals (NAESP) developed the ELCC standards from ISLLC, adding one standard on the basis of a year-long internship. The following are the ELCC standards:

Standard 1. A school district leader who has the knowledge and ability to promote the success of all students by facilitating the development, articulation, implementation, and stewardship of a school or district vision of learning that is supported by the school community;

Standard 2. A school district leader who has the knowledge and ability to promote the success of all students by promoting a positive school culture, providing an effective instructional program, applying best practices to student learning, and designing comprehensive professional growth plans for staff;

Standard 3. A school district leader who has the knowledge and ability to promote the success of all students by managing the organization, operations, and resources in a way that promotes a safe, efficient, and effective learning environment;

Standard 4. A school district leader who has the knowledge and ability to promote the success of all students by collaborating with families and other community members, responding to diverse community interests and needs, and mobilizing community resources;

Standard 5. A school district leader who has the knowledge and ability to promote the success of all students by acting with integrity and fairness and in an ethical manner;

Standard 6. A school district leader who has the knowledge and ability to promote the success of all students by understanding, responding to, and influencing the larger political, social, economic, legal, and cultural context; and

Standard 7. The internship provides significant opportunities for candidates to synthesize and apply the knowledge and practice and develop the skills identified in standards 1–6 through substantial, sustained, standards-based work in real settings, planned and guided cooperatively by the institution and school district personnel for graduate credit.

In table 6.1, the alignment of the standards (knowledge, skills, and dispositions) of ISLLC and ELCC are presented.

| ISLLC Standards | | ELCC Standards | |
| --- | --- | --- | --- |
| **Standard 1: A school administrator is an educational leader who promotes the success of all students facilitating the development, articulation, implementation, and stewardship of a vision of learning that is shared and supported by the school community (Visionary Leadership)** | | **Standard 1.0: Candidates who complete the program are educational leaders who have the knowledge and ability to promote the success of all students by facilitating the development, articulation, implementation, and stewardship of a school or district vision of learning supported by the school community.** | |
| K 1.1 | Learning goals in a pluralistic society. | 1.1 Develop a Vision | a. Candidates develop a vision of learning for a school that promotes the success of all students. |
| K 1.2 | The principles of developing and implementing strategic plans. | | |
| K 1.3 | Systems theory. | | b. Candidates base this vision on relevant knowledge and theories, including but not limited to an understanding of learning goals in a pluralistic society, the diversity of learners and learners' needs, schools as interactive social and cultural systems, and social and organizational change. |
| K 1.4 | Information sources, data collection, and data analysis strategies. | | |
| K 1.5 | Effective communications. | | |
| K 1.6 | Effective consensus-building and negotiation skills. | | |
| D 1.1 | The educability of all students. | | |
| D 1.2 | A school vision of high standards of learning. | | |
| D 1.3 | Continuous school improvement. | | |
| D 1.4 | The inclusion of all members of the school community. | 1.2 Articulate a Vision | a. Candidates demonstrate the ability to articulate the components of this vision for a school and the leadership processes necessary to implement and support the vision. |
| D 1.5 | Ensuring that students have the knowledge, skills, and values needed to become successful adults. | | |
| D 1.6 | A willingness to continuously examine one's own assumptions, beliefs, and practices. | | |
| D 1.7 | Doing the work required for high level of personal and organizational performance. | | b. Candidates demonstrate the ability to use data-based research strategies and strategic planning processes that focus on student learning to inform the development of a vision, drawing on relevant information sources such as student assessment results, student and family demographic data, and an analysis of community needs. |
| P 1.1 | The vision and mission of the school are effectively communicated to staff, parents, students, and community members. | | |
| P 1.2 | The vision and mission are communicated through the use of symbols, ceremonies, stories, and similar activities. | | |
| P 1.3 | The core beliefs of the school vision are modeled for all stakeholders. | | |
| P 1.4 | The vision is developed with and among stakeholders. | | |
| P 1.5 | The contributions of school community members to the realization of the vision are recognized and celebrated. | | c. Candidates demonstrate the ability to communicate the vision to staff, parents, students, and community members through the use of symbols, ceremonies, stories, and other activities. |
| P 1.6 | Progress toward the vision and mission is communicated to all stakeholders. | | |
| P 1.7 | The school community is involved in school improvement efforts. | | |
| P 1.8 | The vision and goals for student learning shapes the educational programs, plans, and actions. | | |
| P 1.9 | An implementation plan is developed in which objectives and strategies to achieve the vision and goals for student learning are clearly articulated. | 1.3 Implement a Vision | a. Candidates can formulate the initiatives necessary to motivate staff, students, and families to achieve the school's vision. |
| P 1.10 | Assessment data related to student learning are used to develop the school vision and goals. | | |

| | | | |
|---|---|---|---|
| P 1.11 | Relevant demographic data pertaining to students and their families are used in developing the school mission and goals. | | b. Candidates develop plans and processes for implementing the vision (e.g., articulating the vision and related goals, encouraging challenging standards, facilitating collegiality and teamwork, structuring significant work, ensuring appropriate use of student assessments, providing autonomy, supporting innovation, delegating responsibility, developing leadership in others, and securing needed resources |
| P 1.12 | Barriers to achieving the vision are identified, clarified. and addressed. | | |
| P 1.13 | Needed resources are sought and obtained to support the implementation of the school mission and goals. | | |
| P 1.14 | Existing resources are used in support of the vision and goals. | | |
| P 1.15 | The vision, mission, and implementation plans are regularly monitored, evaluated and revised. | | |
| | | 1.4 Steward a Vision | a. Candidates demonstrate an understanding of the role effective communication skills play in building a shared commitment to the vision. |
| | | | b. Candidates design or adopt a system for using data-based research strategies to regularly monitor, evaluate, and revise the vision. |
| | | | c. Candidates assume stewardship of the vision through various methods. |
| | | 1.5 Promote Community Involvement in the Vision | a. Candidates demonstrate the ability to involve community members in the realization of the vision and in related school improvement efforts. |
| | | | b. Candidates acquire and demonstrate the skills needed to communicate effectively with all stakeholders about implementation of the vision |

| Standard 2: school administrator is an educational leader who promotes the success of all students by advocating, nurturing, and sustaining a school culture and instructional program conducive to student learning and staff professional development. (Instructional Leadership) | | Standard 2.0: Candidates who complete the program are educational leaders who have the knowledge and ability to promote the success of all students by promoting a positive school culture, providing an effective instructional program, applying best practice to student learning, and designing comprehensive professional growth plans for staff. | |
|---|---|---|---|
| K2.1 | Student growth and development | 2.1 Promote Positive School Culture | a. Candidates assess school culture using multiple methods and implement context-appropriate strategies that capitalize on the diversity (e.g., population, language, disability, gender, race, socio-economic) of the school community to improve school programs and culture. |
| K 2.2 | Applied learning theories | | |
| K 2.3 | Applied motivational theories | | |
| K 2.4 | Curriculum design, implementation, evaluation, and refinement | | |
| K 2.5 | Principles of effective instruction | 2.2 Provide Effective Instructional Program | a. Candidates demonstrate the ability to facilitate activities that apply principles of effective instruction to improve instructional practices and curricular materials. |
| K 2.6 | Measurement, evaluation, and assessment strategies | | |
| K 2.7 | Diversity and its meaning for educational programs | | b. Candidates demonstrate the ability to make recommendations regarding the design, implementation, and evaluation of a curriculum that fully accommodates learners' diverse needs. |
| K 2.8 | Adult learning and professional development models | | |
| K 2.9 | The change process for systems, organizations, and individuals | | |
| K 2.10 | The role of technology in promoting student learning and professional growth. | | c. Candidates demonstrate the ability to use and promote technology and information systems to enrich curriculum and instruction, to monitor instructional practices and provide staff the assistance needed for improvement. |
| K 2.11 | School cultures and instructional program are conducive to student learning and staff professional development | | |
| D.2.1 | The fundamental purpose of schooling | | |
| D 2.2 | The proposition that all students can learn | | |
| D 2.3 | The variety of ways in which students can learn | 2.3 Apply Best Practice to Student Learning | a. Candidates demonstrate the ability to assist school personnel in understanding and applying best practices for student |
| D 2.4 | Life long learning for self and others | | |
| D 2.5 | Professional development as an integral part of school improvement | | |

| | | | |
|---|---|---|---|
| D 2.6 | The benefits that diversity brings to the school community | | learning. |
| D 2.7 | A safe and supportive learning environment | | b. Candidates apply human development theory, proven learning and motivational theories, and concern for diversity to the learning process. |
| D 2.8 | Preparing students to be contributing members of society | | |
| D 2.9 | The partnership and collaboration with and among staff. | | |
| P 2.1 | All individuals are treated with fairness, dignity, and respect | | |
| P 2.2 | Professional development promotes a focus on student learning consistent with the school vision and goals | | c. Candidates demonstrate an understanding of how to use appropriate research strategies to promote an environment for improved student achievement. |
| P 2.3 | Students and staff feel valued and important | | |
| P 2.4 | The responsibilities and contributions of each individual are acknowledged | | |
| P 2.5 | Barriers to student learning are identified, clarified, and addressed | | |
| P 2.6 | Diversity is considered in developing learning experiences | 2.4 Design Comprehensive Professional Growth Plans | a. Candidates design and demonstrate an ability to implement well-planned, context-appropriate professional development programs based on reflective practice and research on student learning consistent with the school vision and goals. |
| P 2.7 | Life long learning is encouraged and modeled | | |
| P 2.8 | There is a culture of high expectations for self, student, and staff performance | | |
| P 2.9 | Technologies are used in teaching and learning | | |
| P 2.10 | Student and staff accomplishments are recognized and celebrated | | |
| P 2.11 | Multiple opportunities to learn are available to all students | | |
| P 2.12 | The school is organized and aligned for success | | b. Candidates demonstrate the ability to use strategies such as observations, collaborative reflection, and adult learning strategies to form comprehensive professional growth plans with teachers and other school personnel. |
| P 2.13 | Curricular, co-curricular, and extra-curricular programs are designed, implemented, evaluated, and refined | | |
| P 2.14 | Curriculum decisions are based on research, expertise of teachers, and the recommendations of learned societies | | |
| P 2.15 | The school culture and climate and assessed on a regular basis | | c. Candidates develop and implement personal professional growth plans that reflect a commitment to life-long learning. |
| P 2.16 | A variety of sources of information are used to make decisions | | |
| P 2.17 | Student learning is assessed using variety of techniques | | |
| P 2.18 | Multiple sources of information regarding performance are used by staff and students | | |
| P 2.19 | A variety of supervisory and evaluation models is employed | | |
| P 2.20 | Pupil personnel programs are developed to meet the needs of students and their families. | | |

| Standard 3: A school administrator is an educational leader who promotes the success of all students by ensuring management of the organization, operations, and resources for a safe, efficient, and effective learning environment. (Organizational Leadership) | | Standard 3.0: Candidates who complete the program are educational leaders who have the knowledge and ability to promote the success of all students by managing the organization, operations, and resources in a way that promotes a safe, efficient, and effective learning environment. | |
|---|---|---|---|
| K 3.1 | Theories and models of organizations and the principles of organizational development | 3.1 Manage the Organization | a. Candidates demonstrate the ability to optimize the learning environment for all students by applying appropriate models and principles of organizational development and management, including research and data driven decision-making with attention to indicators of equity, effectiveness, and efficiency. |
| K 3.2 | Operational procedures at the school and district level | | |
| K 3.3 | Principles and issues relating to school safety and security | | |
| K 3.4 | Human resources management and development | | |
| K 3.5 | Principles and issues relating to fiscal operations of school management | | b. Candidates develop plans of action for focusing on effective organization and management of fiscal, human, and material resources, giving priority to student learning, safety, curriculum, and instruction. |
| K 3.6 | Principles and issues relating to school facilities and use of space | | |
| K 3.7 | Legal issues impacting school operations | | |
| K 3.8 | Current technologies that support management functions. | | c. Candidates demonstrate an ability to manage time effectively and deploy financial and human resources in ways that promote student achievement. |
| D 3.1 | Making management decisions to enhance learning and teaching | | |
| D 3.2 | Taking risks to improve schools | | |
| D 3.3 | Trusting people and their judgments | | |
| D 3.4 | Accepting responsibility | 3.2 Manage Operations | a. Candidates demonstrate the ability to involve staff in conducting operations and setting priorities using appropriate and effective needs assessment, research-based data, and group process skills to build consensus, communicate, and resolve conflicts in order to align resources with the organizational vision. |
| D 3.5 | High quality standards, expectations, and performances | | |
| D 3.6 | Involving stakeholders in management processes | | |
| D 3.7 | A safe environment. | | |
| P 3.1 | Knowledge of learning, teaching, and student development is used to inform management decisions | | b. Candidates develop communications plans for staff |
| P 3.2 | Operational procedures are designed and managed to maximize opportunities for successful learning | | |

| | | | |
|---|---|---|---|
| P 3.3 | Emerging trends are recognized, studied, and managed to maximize opportunities for successful learning | | that includes opportunities for staff to develop their family and community collaboration skills. |
| P 3.4 | Operational plans and procedures to achieve the vision and goals of the school are in place | | |
| P 3.5 | Collective bargaining and other contractual agreements related to the school are effectively managed | | c. Candidates demonstrate an understanding of how to apply legal principles to promote educational equity and provide a safe, effective, and efficient facilities. |
| P 3.6 | The school plant, equipment, and support systems operate safely, efficiently, and effectively | | |
| P 3.7 | Time is managed to maximize attainment of organizational goals | | |
| P 3.8 | Potential problems and opportunities are identified | 3.3 Manage Resources | a. Candidates use problem-solving skills and knowledge of strategic, long-range, and operational planning (including applications of technology) in the effective, legal, and equitable use of fiscal, human, and material resource allocation and alignment that focuses on teaching and learning. |
| P 3.9 | Problems are confronted and resolved in a timely manner | | |
| P 3.10 | Financial, human, and material resources are aligned to the goals of schools | | |
| P 3.11 | The school acts entrepreneur ally to support continuous improvement | | |
| P 3.12 | Organizational systems are regularly monitored and modified as needed | | |
| P 3.13 | Stakeholders are involved in decisions affecting schools | | |
| P 3.14 | Responsibility is shared to maximize ownership and accountability | | b. Candidates creatively seek new resources to facilitate learning. |
| P 3.15 | Effective problem-framing and problem-solving skills are used | | c. Candidates apply and assess current technologies for school management, business procedures, and scheduling. |
| P 3.16 | Effective conflict resolution skills are used | | |
| P 3.17 | Effective group-process and consensus building skills are used | | |
| P 3.18 | Effective communications skills are used | | |
| P 3.19 | There is effective use of technology to manage school operations | | |
| P 3.20 | Fiscal resources of the school and managed responsibly, efficiently, and effectively | | |
| P 3.21 | A safe, clean, and aesthetically pleasing school environment is created and maintained | | |
| P 3.22 | Human resource functions support the attainment of school goals | | |
| P 3.23 | Confidentiality and privacy of school records are maintained. | | |

| Standard 4: A school administrator is an educational leader who promotes the success of all students by collaborating with families and community members, responding to diverse community interests and needs, and mobilizing community resources. (Collaborative Leadership) | | Standard 4.0: Candidates who complete the program are educational leaders who have the knowledge and ability to promote the success of all students by collaborating with families and other community members, responding to diverse community interests and needs, and mobilizing community resources. | |
|---|---|---|---|
| K 4.1 | Emerging issues and trends that potentially impact the school community | 4.1 Collaborate with Families and Other Community Members | a. Candidates demonstrate an ability to bring together the resources of family members and the community to positively affect student learning. |
| K 4.2 | The conditions and dynamics of the diverse school community | | b. Candidates demonstrate an ability to involve families in the education of their children based on the belief that families have the best interests of their children in mind. |
| K 4.3 | Community resources | | |
| K 4.4 | Community relations and marketing strategies and processes | | c. Candidates demonstrate the ability to use public information and research-based knowledge of issues and trends to collaborate with families and community members. |
| K 4.5 | Successful models of school, family, business, community, government, and higher education partnerships. | | |
| D 4.1 | Schools operating as an integral part of a larger community | | d. Candidates apply an understanding of community relations models, marketing strategies and processes, data-based decision-making, and communications theory to create frameworks for school, family, business, community, government, and higher education partnerships. |
| D 4.2 | Collaboration and communication with families | | |
| D 4.3 | Involvement of families and other stakeholders in school decision-making processes | | |
| D 4.4 | The proposition that diversity enriches the school | | e. Candidates develop various methods of outreach aimed at business, religious, political, and service organizations. |
| D 4.5 | Families as partners in the education of their children | | |
| D 4.6 | The proposition that families have the best interests of their children in mind | | f. Candidates demonstrate the ability to involve families and other stakeholders in school decision-making processes, reflecting an understanding that schools are an integral part of the larger community. |
| D 4.7 | Resources of the family and community needing to be brought to bear on the education of students | | |
| D 4.8 | An informed public. | | g. Candidates demonstrate the ability to collaborate with community agencies to integrate health, social, and other services. |
| P 4.1 | High visibility, active involvement, and communication with the larger community is a priority | | |
| P 4.2 | Relationships with community leaders are identified and nurtured | | h. Candidates develop a comprehensive program of community relations and demonstrate the ability to work with the media. |
| P 4.3 | Information about families and community concerns, expectations, and needs is used regularly | 4.2 Respond to Community Interests | a. Candidates demonstrate active involvement within the community, including interactions with individuals |
| P 4.4 | There is outreach to different business, religious, | | |

| | | and Needs | and groups with conflicting perspectives. |
|---|---|---|---|
| | political, and service agencies and organizations | | |
| P 4.5 | Credence is given to individuals and groups whose values and opinions may conflict | | b. Candidates demonstrate the ability to use appropriate assessment strategies and research methods to understand and accommodate diverse school and community conditions and dynamics. |
| P 4.6 | The school and community serve one another as resources | | |
| P 4.7 | Available community resources are secured to help the school solve problems and achieve goals | | c. Candidates provide leadership to programs serving students with special and exceptional needs. |
| P 4.8 | Partnerships are established with area businesses, and institutions of higher education, and community groups to strengthen programs and support school goals | | d. Candidates demonstrate the ability to capitalize on the diversity (cultural, ethnic, racial, economic, and special interest groups) of the school community to improve school programs and meet the diverse needs of all students. |
| P 4.9 | Community family youth services are integrated with school programs | 4.3 Mobilize Community Resources | a. Candidates demonstrate an understanding of and ability to use community resources, including youth services, to support student achievement, solve school problems, and achieve school goals. |
| P 4.10 | Community stakeholders are treated equitably | | |
| P 4.11 | Diversity is recognized and valued | | b. Candidates demonstrate how to use school resources and social service agencies to serve the community. |
| P 4.12 | Effective media relations are developed and maintained | | |
| P 4.13 | A comprehensive program of community relations is established | | c. Candidates demonstrate an understanding of ways to use public resources and funds appropriately and effectively to encourage communities to provide new resources to address emerging student problems. |
| P 4.14 | Public resources and funds are used appropriately and wisely | | |
| P 4.15 | Community collaboration is modeled for staff | | |
| P 4.16 | Opportunities for staff to develop collaborative skills are provided. | | |

| Standard 5: A school administrator is an educational leader who promotes the success of all students by acting with integrity, fairness, and in an ethical manner. (Ethical Leadership) | | Standard 5.0: Candidates who complete the program are educational leaders who have the knowledge and ability to promote the success of all students by acting with integrity, fairly, and in an ethical manner. | |
|---|---|---|---|
| K 5.1 | The purpose of education and the role of leadership in modern society | 5.1 Acts with Integrity | a. Candidates demonstrate a respect for the rights of others with regard to confidentiality and dignity and engage in honest interactions. |
| K 5.2 | Various ethical frameworks and perspectives on ethics | | |
| K 5.3 | The values of the diverse school community | 5.2 Acts Fairly | a. Candidates demonstrate the ability to combine impartiality, sensitivity to student diversity, and ethical considerations in their interactions with others. |
| K 5.4 | Professional codes and ethics | | |
| K 5.5 | The philosophy and history of education. | | |
| D 5.1 | The ideal of the common good | 5.3 Acts Ethically | a. Candidates make and explain decisions based upon ethical and legal principles. |
| D 5.2 | The principles in the Bill of Rights | | |
| D 5.3 | The right of every student to a free, quality education | | |
| D 5.4 | Bringing ethical principles to the decision-making process | | |
| D 5.5 | Subordinating one's own interest to the good of the school community | | |
| D 5.6 | Accepting the consequences for upholding one's principles and actions | | |
| D 5.7 | Using the influence of ones office constructively and productively in the Service of all students and their families | | |
| D 5.8 | Development of a caring school community. | | |
| P 5.1 | Examines personal and professional values | | |
| P 5.2 | Demonstrates a personal and professional code of ethics | | |
| P 5.3 | Demonstrates values, beliefs, and attitudes, that inspires others to higher levels of performance | | |
| P 5.4 | Serves as a role model | | |
| P 5.5 | Accepts responsibility for school operations | | |

| | |
|---|---|
| P 5.6 | Considers the impact of one's administrative practices on others |
| P 5.7 | Uses the influence of the office to enhance the educational program rather than the personal gain |
| P 5.8 | Treats people fairly, equitably, and with dignity and respect |
| P 5.9 | Protects the rights and confidentiality of students and staff |
| P 5.10 | Demonstrates appreciation for and sensitivity to the diversity in the school community |
| P 5.11 | Expects that others in the school community will demonstrate integrity and exercise ethical behavior |
| P 5.12 | Opens the school to public scrutiny |
| P 5.13 | Applies laws and procedures fairly wisely, and considerably. |

| Standard 6: A school administrator is an educational leader who promotes the success of all students by understanding, responding to, and influencing the larger political, social, economic, legal, and cultural context. (Political Leadership) | | Standard 6.0: Candidates who complete the program are educational leaders who have the knowledge and ability to promote the success of all students by understanding, responding to, and influencing the larger political, social, economic, legal, and cultural context. | |
|---|---|---|---|
| K 6.1 | Principles of representative governance that under grid the system of American schools | 6.1 Understand the Larger Context | a. Candidates act as informed consumers of educational theory and concepts appropriate to school context and can demonstrate the ability to apply appropriate research methods to a school context. |
| K 6.2 | The role of public education in developing and renewing a democratic society and an economically productive nation | | |
| K 6.3 | The law as related to education and schooling | | |
| K 6.4 | The political, social, cultural, and economic systems and processes that impact schools | | b. Candidates demonstrate the liability to explain how the legal and political systems and institutional framework of schools have shaped a school and community, as well as the opportunities available to children and families in a particular school. |
| K 6.5 | Models and strategies of change and conflict resolution as applied to the larger political, social, cultural, and economic contexts of schooling | | |
| K 6.6 | Global issues and forces affecting teaching and learning | | |
| K 6.7 | The dynamics of policy development and advocacy under our democratic political system | | c. Candidates demonstrate the ability to analyze the complex causes of poverty and other disadvantages and their effects on families, communities, children, and learning. |
| K 6.8 | The importance of diversity and equity in a democratic society. | | |
| D 6.1 | Education as a key to opportunity and social mobility | | |
| D 6.2 | Recognizing a variety of ideas, values, and cultures | | d. Candidates demonstrate an understanding of the policies, laws, and regulations enacted by local, state, and federal authorities that affect schools, especially those that might improve educational and social opportunities. |
| D 6.3 | Importance of a continuing dialogue with other decision makers affecting education | | |
| D 6.4 | Actively participating in the political and policy-making affecting education | | |
| D 6.5 | Using legal systems to protect student rights and improve student opportunities. | | e. Candidates demonstrate the ability to describe the economic factors shaping a local community and the effects economic factors have on local schools. |
| P 6.1 | The environment in which school operates is influenced on behalf of students and their families | | |
| P 6.2 | Communication occurs among school community concerning trends, issues, and potential changes in the environment in which the school operates | | f. Candidates demonstrate the ability to analyze and describe the cultural diversity in a school |
| P 6.3 | There is ongoing dialogue with representatives of diverse community groups | | |

| P 6.4 | The school community works within the framework of policies, laws, and regulations enacted by local, state, and federal authorities | | community. |
|---|---|---|---|
| | | | g. Candidates can describe community norms and values and how they relate to the role of the school in promoting social justice. |
| P 6.5 | Public policy is shaped to provide quality education for students | | |
| P 6.6 | Lines of communications are developed with decision makers outside school community. | | h. Candidates demonstrate the ability to explain various theories of change and conflict resolution and the appropriate application of those models to specific communities |
| | | 6.2 Respond to the Larger Context | a. Candidates demonstrate the ability to communicate with members of a school community concerning trends, issues, and potential changes in the environment in which the school operates, including maintenance of an ongoing dialogue with representatives of diverse community groups. |
| | | 6.3 Influence the Larger Context | a. Candidates demonstrate the ability to engage students, parents, and other members of the community in advocating for adoption of improved policies and laws. |
| | | | b. Candidates apply their understanding of the larger political, social, economic, legal, and cultural context to develop activities and policies that benefit students and their families. |
| | | | c. Candidates advocate for policies and programs that promote equitable learning opportunities and success for all students, regardless of socioeconomic background, ethnicity, gender, disability, or other individual characteristics. |

| | Standard 7.0: Internship. The internship provides significant opportunities for candidates to synthesize and apply the knowledge and practice and develop the skills identified in Standards 1-6 through substantial, sustained, standards-based work in real settings, planned and guided cooperatively by the institution and school district personnel for graduate credit. | |
|---|---|---|
| | 7.1 Substantial | a. Candidates demonstrate the ability to accept genuine responsibility for leading, facilitating, and making decisions typical of those made by educational leaders. The experience(s) should provide interns with substantial responsibilities that increase over time in amount and complexity and involve direct interaction and involvement with staff, students, parents, and community leaders.<br><br>b. Each candidate should have a minimum of six months (or equivalent, see note below) of fulltime internship experience. |
| | 7.2 Sustained | a. Candidates participate in planned intern activities during the entire course of the program, including an extended period of time near the conclusion of the program to allow for candidate application of knowledge and skills on a full-time basis. |
| | 7.3 Standards-based | a. Candidates apply skills and knowledge articulated in these standards as well as state and local standards for educational leaders.<br><br>b. Experiences are designed to accommodate candidates' individual needs. |

| | 7.4 Real Settings | a. Candidates' experiences occur in multiple settings that allow for the demonstration of a wide range of relevant knowledge and skills. |
| | | b. Candidates' experiences include work with appropriate community organizations such as social service groups and local businesses. |
| | 7.5 Planned and Guided Cooperatively | a. Candidates' experiences are planned cooperatively by the individual, the site supervisor, and institution personnel to provide inclusion of appropriate opportunities to apply skills, knowledge, and research contained in the standards. These three individuals work together to meet candidate and program needs. |
| | 7.6 Credit | b. Mentors are provided training to guide the candidate during the intern experience |
| | | a. Candidates earn graduate credit for their intern experience. |

# STANDARD 1

Standard 1 (The Vision of Learning). A school administrator is an educational leader who promotes the success of all students by facilitating the development, articulation, implementation, and stewardship of a vision of learning that is shared and supported by the school community.

Many scholars have noted the importance of leaders in possessing visions for organizations, particularly school leaders. According to Kowalski (2010),[3] a vision describes the future state of schools, accounting for the mission and embracing the philosophy of the school. It is important for practitioners to strive for achievement of the vision; the vision must also be vivid and concrete (Blankstein 2010).[4] Several perspectives of vision are noted in the literature as early as the 1990s.

Mental picture or image, future orientation, and aspects of goals and direction were included in perspectives of vision both in the 1990s and currently. In addition to the multiple perspectives of vision that are frequently referred to as vision statements, there are differing philosophies about the visioning process, specifically, the role of the leader in the visioning process and the need to have written visions as compared to unwritten visions. Fritz[5]

(1996) noted that written visions may become political compromises, and Conley and colleagues[6] (1998) suggested that some schools progress well with visions before articulating them in writing.

The school leaders play critical roles in school improvement. And vision statements are commonly viewed as essential elements of school improvement planning and strategic planning primarily because of the emphases of the visions on what the schools will look like. Rakiz and Swanson (2000) suggest that an initial step toward school improvement is for the leaders to set visions. In 1995, Carr[7] suggested that the visions originate in the mind of the leaders, and it is a critical quality of leadership in which the leaders communicate and obtain support from teachers and stakeholders. There are current emphases in the visioning process on the role of stakeholder involvement in development— including teachers, parents, and in some instances students. *who are stakeholders?*

Mission and vision have been used interchangeably. And Kowalski[8] (2012) notes the need to distinguish between mission, vision, and philosophy. The vision should not be done in isolation of the mission; however, mission involves a purpose, what should be accomplished. Visions should include what schools look like in meeting their missions. Ubben and colleagues (2011)[9] suggest that the vision of the school is linked to the quality of a school primarily because the vision provides a sense of direction. The findings of a qualitative study conducted by Kose (2008, March)[10] suggest that school leaders play critical roles in the visioning process. Theorists have noted the complexity of the visioning process along with the tendency for the process to be misinterpreted. Blankstein[11] (2010) outlines five criteria for effective visions:

1. The vision is developed with collective input from all stakeholders, and it is shared by all.
2. It is imaginable and feasible; all stakeholders can picture a school community such as the one described.
3. It is clearly desirable and in the interest of all to bring about the teaching and learning community.
4. The vision is both specific enough to provide guidance for decisions and goals setting and flexible enough to remain viable under changing conditions.
5. The vision is clear and easily communicated, either in writing or in casual conversation.

*What 3 variables hamper the vision proc.*

Kowalski[12] (2012) suggests that the following three variables hamper the visioning process: uncertainty, risk, and conflict. The uncertainty in the process is linked to decision making. Because of the diminished certainty regarding the future, there are challenges with decision making. Obviously, there is always the potential for a decision to be detrimental, which brings in the risk factor.

As previously alluded to, there is emerging heightened emphasis on involving stakeholders in schools with school improvement and other kinds of decision making. Involving more individuals increases the potential for conflict. Disagreements are inevitable; challenges present opportunities for growth in organizations. There is an opportunity to build positive school cultures through involving staff members. The issue of school culture (establishing high expectations for teaching and learning) will be revisited as linked to several of the standards.

There is direct alignment of the vision to school culture through school improvement. As previously cited, visions are viable to school improvement. The leader plays a critical role in monitoring, assessing, and improving school culture pertinent to school improvement. The findings of the effective schools research suggest that effective schools have strong cultures. The concept of shared decision making was identified by Phillips and Wagner[13] (2003) as an element for positive cultures.

Shared decision making has direct implications for shared leadership, which involves empowering the pertinent employees in decision making. Protecting what is important is another concept presented by Phillips and Wagner[14] (2003) as an indicator of strong school cultures. This requires buy-in of the vision by staff. Therefore, there is a sense that the vision must be shared. Ownership in the vision is vital.

Phillips and Wagner[15] (2003) also suggest that the leaders of positive school cultures "carry the vision for the group." Ineffective leaders are unable to support others, "join others in whining," view only the problems of the work environment, and model "scapegoating" by blaming students, parents, the board office, or society. Effective leaders also promote efficacy and collegiality in schools. Teachers and staff feel ownership, feel that they can influence important decisions, solve problems, and use their wisdom to create appropriate new approaches—efficacy. Collegiality is promoted by the leader when participants share new educational ideals, have access to ideas on a regular basis, observe others regularly, and coach or teach each other.

The Office of Quality Educators in Louisiana has adopted ISLLC; however, in 2007, prior to the adoption of ISLLC, vision was defined as the school leaders' engaging the school communities in the developing and maintaining student-center visions. This perspective addresses the significant cultural component of the vision addressed in the discussion of the previous paragraphs. The following are the performances that were associated with maintaining a vision:

- work collaboratively with the school community to develop and maintain a shared vision;
- bring the school vision to life by using it to guide decision making about students and instructional programs;
- maintain faculty focus on developing learning experiences that will enable students to prosper in subsequent grades and as adults;
- maintain open communication with the school community and effectively convey high expectations for student learning to the community;
- provide opportunities and support for collaboration, the exchange of ideas, experimentation with innovative teaching strategies, and ongoing school improvement;
- monitor, assess, and revise the school vision and goals as needed; and
- foster the integration of students into mainstream society while valuing diversity.[16]

The cultural component embedded in standard 1 of ISLLC has direct implications for standard 2. Leaders who facilitate positive school cultures also set high expectations for teaching and learning on the part of both the students and other educators in the building. The roles of leaders in nurturing and facilitating "teaching and learning" are components of standard 2. In *Good to Great*, Jim Collins discusses characteristics essential for leadership along with aspects of work environments.

He compares the business sector with the social sector. Collins notes in both sectors the importance of culture. He suggests that there can be constraints in cultures that impact the quality and effectiveness of the work. "Getting the right people on the bus" is the verbiage that he uses as linked to the role of stakeholder involvement.[17] Therefore, it is important to have people engaged in the environment to obtain the most positive results.


## STANDARD 2


Standard 2 (The Culture of Teaching and Learning) focuses on advocating, nurturing, and sustaining a school culture and instructional program conducive to student learning and staff professional growth.

Gray (2009, January)[18] suggested that NCLB is grounded in an effort to influence the curriculum in classrooms, and there is the realization that teachers alone cannot create the conditions to meet the requirements of standardized testing and accountability. The role of the school leader as an instructional leader is strongly embedded in standard 2. Prior to the Soviet Union launching Sputnik and shortly after World War II, administration preparation programs focused on management skills because of the valuing of efficiency in management.

Congress began to focus more on curriculum after Sputnik, particularly mathematics and science. Over time, there has been a heightened interest in curriculum, and an unintended consequence of NCLB has been a redefinition of the principal's role as an instructional leader. Emphases have also been placed on changing obsolete principal-preparation programs and developing the concepts of shared vision and the knowledge and abilities necessary for instructional leadership.

The work of an instructional leader is in the classroom, promoting instructional programs and professional development while maintaining a culture of high expectations for teaching and learning. Good teaching will not occur in a vacuum; Ubben and colleagues[19] identify five premises that are fundamental in promoting the qualities of great cultures: schooling occurs in group context; learning occurs best in an orderly environment; an orderly environment can be best achieved by policies and strategies that promote self-regulation of behavior rather than policies and strategies; the environment is enhanced when the staff behaves in an orderly and internally controlled way; and the rules to guide behavior should be simple, well known, and continuously reinforced.

The leaders have to work at building the culture through nurturing and building relationships. Connors (2003)[20] suggests on the bases of practical experiences as a school leader that the school leader has to constantly monitor and assess the culture and engage in dispositions to promote positivism in cultures in schools.

Hoy and Miskel[21] (2008) present three major categorizations of leadership perspectives—transformational, transactional, and contingency. Transformational leadership is an expansion of transactional. Transactional is trading one thing for another; transformational is more focused on change. The contingency theory has two hypotheses. First, leadership behavior is impacted by characteristics of situations, traits, and skills of leaders. Second, situational factors impact the effectiveness of the leader. Instructional leadership is one of the five contingency models. Hoy and Miskel (2008) suggested that instructional leadership evolved from "simple heroic conception."[22]

Ten attributes identified by Smith and Andrews (1989) critical to instructional leadership are

1. Places priority on curriculum and instruction issues;
2. Is dedicated to the goals of the school and school district;
3. Is able to rally and mobilize resources to accomplish the goals of the district and school;

4. Creates a climate of high expectations in the school, characterized by a tone of respect for teachers, students, parents, and the community;
5. Functions as a leader with direct involvement in instructional policy;
6. Continually monitors student progress toward school achievement and teacher effectiveness;
7. Demonstrates commitment to academic goals, shown by the ability to develop and articulate a clear vision or long-term goals for the school;
8. Effectively consults with others by involving the faculty and other groups in the school decision processes;
9. Effectively and efficiently mobilizes resources such as materials, time, and support to enable the school and its personnel to most effectively meet academic goals; and
10. Recognizes time as a scarce resource and creates order and discipline by minimizing factors that may disrupt the learning process.

As previously addressed, instructional leadership has direct implications for the classroom. Zepeda (2003)[23] presents a model of how instructional leadership should be aligned with classroom observations and professional development. This model, presented in figure 6.1, was also presented in *The Relevance of Instructional Leadership*.

In *The Relevance of Instructional Leadership*, Jones (2011) explains that the clinical model should be coupled with differentiated supervision. In differentiated supervision, the teacher has the autonomy to decide additional mechanisms to be evaluated on supplementary to the observation. The results of the observations will dictate to the principal the kinds of skills/competencies the teacher is proficient with or lacking proficiency in. When teachers are proficient, they can serve as mentors or leaders of faculty study groups. When they are lacking proficiency, teachers need to be mentored or placed in groups to be assisted.

Mentoring and grouping are tools that principals can use as a result of evaluations to help build skills within the faculty. The mentoring and/or grouping should lead to professional and/or staff development; the staff development should obviously be aligned with the results of the observation. Teachers will need staff development in areas where they are less proficient. The staff development should also lead to individual goal setting—all of which the principal as an evaluator of teaching facilitates. The cycle begins again with the next observation.

The facilitation of effective teaching and meaningful professional development are emphasized in the model. Providing opportunities for effective professional development is one manner for school leaders to build learning communities. Blankstein (2010) emphasizes in *Failure Is Not an Option* that

**Figure 6.1** Model of Unifying Instructional Supervision (Instructional Leadership,) Classroom Observations & Professional Development

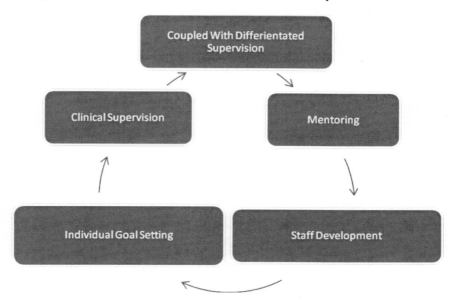

an imperative challenge for school leaders in obtaining and sustaining success is establishing professional learning communities; their establishment is vital to school improvement.

## STANDARD 3

Standard 3 (Management of Learning) revolves around ensuring management of the organization, operations, and resources for a safe, efficient, and effective learning environment.

Although great emphases are placed on the role of school leaders as instructional leaders, it is vital for the leaders to be knowledgeable about efficient management techniques and strategies. Furthermore, many managerial decisions are critical to facilitating effective teaching and aspects of the learning environment. For instance, both knowledge and effective use of knowledge about budgeting, human resources, and other resources are advantageous to staffing schools with the pertinent teachers and other individuals for the most appropriate classrooms, purchasing materials and equipment, funding professional development activities, and maximizing the use of resources that are available.

As a matter of fact, a model provided by the Chicago Public Schools titled "Five Fundamentals of Success" identifies resource management as critical to instructional leadership and whole-school improvement. The key indicators of excellence in resource management are

- the instructional leadership team effectively allocates and manages the school resources—people, time, funds, and materials—to address school priorities and students' needs;
- the school community evaluates and plans school programs and policies based on their contributions toward reaching school goals; and
- teachers use other staff, classroom volunteers, and family resources at home to maximize the amount of individualized instruction students receive (Chicago Public Schools). [24]

Historically, there have been three major leadership theory shifts. In the early 1900s, the focus of leadership theory was on the organization—scientific management. Administrators were expected to "manage" the goals of the organization. Bureaucracy, chain of command, standardization, hierarchy of control, and efficiency are the verbiage associated with this historical period. In the 1930s, leadership theory shifted its focus to a humanistic perspective—the natural systems perspectives. The goals of the organization were minimized, with emphases on meeting the needs of individuals in the organization. Key concepts associated with the natural systems perspectives include survival, needs, individual social structures, informal norms, and empowerment.

The current shift in leadership theory focuses on balancing the needs of the organization while simultaneously meeting the needs of employees—the open systems perspective. Key concepts associated with open systems include interdependence of the organization and its environment, integration of organizational goals and human needs, and integration of rational and natural features. The "balancing act" obviously requires effective decision making—managerial and leadership skills (Hoy & Miskel 2008). [25]

Ubben and colleagues [26] suggest that "good principal leaders also manage, but they manage with a leadership perspective." Good management is needed to create and maintain environments in schools that are orderly. There have been some research studies on the challenges associated with adult learning and why adult learning can be challenging. We raise the notion because some individuals in work environments will need more direction than others.

Scheduling is typically a managerial task, and there are so many implications for scheduling that can impact the instructional environment—having teachers and staff in the appropriate locations and changing locations in smooth transitions throughout the day. As early as the 1970s and some of the more current findings of effective schools research suggest that a safe and orderly school climate is critical to schools that are effective (Freiberg et al., 1990; Stringfield & Herman, 1996).[27]

Many of the concepts previously discussed or mentioned as managerial tasks have decision-making links—that is, scheduling, budgeting and resource management, and staffing—require decision making. There are multiple decision-making models, and Herbert Simon presents decision making as a managerial task. He suggests that "the task of deciding pervades the entire administrative organization."[28] Based on practical experience, we believe that many of the decisions made by school leaders are done very rapidly, and school leaders develop a repertoire of decision-making experiences as reference points.

In classical decision-making theory, it is assumed that decisions should be totally rational. The optimizing concept is employed; the assumption in the optimizing concept is that the best alternative to address the goals and objectives of the organization is achievable. The sequential steps of the decision-making model are

- a problem is identified;
- goals and objectives are established;
- all the possible alternatives are generated;
- the consequences of each alternative are considered;
- all the alternatives are evaluated in terms of goals and objectives;
- the best alternative is selected, that is, the one that maximizes the goals and objectives; and
- finally, the decision is implemented and evaluated.

The challenges with this model of decision making are obvious. Leaders will not have access to all information, and it is nearly impossible to generate all alternatives. A thorough list of alternatives can be developed, but not all. In addition, as some organizational problems are solved, others will evolve, and there is no single "best way to decide." Furthermore, not all of the organizational decision-making models are rational, and irrationality can be produced in decision-making by stress (Hoy &Miskel, 2008.)[29]

## STANDARD 4

Standard 4 (Relations with Broader Community to Foster Learning) is about collaborating with families and community members, responding to diverse community interests and needs, and mobilizing community resources.

Increased emphases are on the roles of school leaders in gaining stakeholder involvement with many aspects of decision making in schools. Two important stakeholder groups that are acknowledged at greater levels are parents and community entities. In our state, a parental representative is a requirement for/of school improvement teams. Henderson and Berla[30] (1994) suggested that an effective parental/family program provides curriculum to the home, and successful programs must be comprehensive (reaching all families), well planned (specific goals), and long lasting.

Joyce Epstein is a leading parental involvement activist. She suggests that there are six kinds of parental involvement: parenting, communicating, volunteering, learning at home, decision making, and collaborating with the community. With each type of parental involvement, Epstein suggests that there are challenges, redefinitions, and practices to achieve the parental involvement type.

Epstein and other researchers cite the value and benefits of parental and community involvement. Epstein and colleagues[31] (2002) suggest that partnerships can improve school programs, improve school climate, build collegiality among parents, help teachers with their work, provide family services and support, and increase parents' skills and leadership. Research findings also suggest

- most or all families care about their children and desire for them to succeed;
- most or all teachers and administrators would like to involve families; and
- most or all students at all levels—elementary, middle, and high school—desire for their parents to be knowledgeable partners in schools.

According to Epstein and colleagues[32] (2002), there are several factors that can impact and promote effective community and parental involvement. One of the factors is the school principal. Principals have to facilitate support for community involvement. The concept of building positivism in the culture has been addressed as pertinent to both ISLLC standards 1 and 2. As it relates to standard 4, the school leaders must demonstrate to parents and community entities high commitment to learning, a welcoming school climate, and two-way communication with potential community partners about their involvement.

## STANDARD 5

Standard 5 (Integrity, Fairness, and Ethics in Learning) deals with acting with integrity, with fairness, and in an ethical manner.

School enrollments are growing rapidly, and the populations of schools have become much more diverse. As early as 1992, Roland Martin[33] suggested that school populations were changing dramatically. Administrators, teachers, and school staffs must address diversity issues in decision making, organization and management, and curriculum and instruction issues. As all school staff members address diversity issues in all of the decision-making areas, the staff must be fair—decisions should not be made accounting for biases, likes, or dislikes. The decisions of school staff should reflect the best decision for the school and individuals directly impacted by the decisions.

Historically, there were primarily two races (African American and European white) of students enrolled in American schools. Presently, American schools are filled with students of many national origins, including Hispanic and Asian populations. In addition to ethnic diversities, schools are more academically and socially diverse. Principals and teachers must address the needs of all student populations as well as promote positive interactions among students and staff.

Before ISLLC was adopted in Louisiana, the previous *Standards for School Principals* in Louisiana (SSPL) also had a standard that addressed professional ethics, standard 7. It was defined as the principal demonstrating honesty, integrity, and fairness to guide school programs in an ethical manner. Modeling the dispositions is important for every standard but specifically important for ethics. The necessary dispositions for ethics included being accurate in providing information while respecting others, caring for the feelings of others, principled action in upholding the substance of laws, policies, regulations, and procedures, and using the influence of the principalship constructively and productively in the service of all students.[34]

How effectively an administrator as well as other staff members exhibit ethics can affect the climate of the school, management, discipline issues, and more importantly teaching and learning. If a teacher feels that the principal is consistently unfair in the assignment of the class loads, this could affect the teacher's productivity—cause the teacher to share the perception with other colleagues. Eventually, staff morale can be impacted negatively, which then leads to a negative impact on student learning. The fair treatment of students becomes critical for administrators as well as teachers; students are very sensitive to inequities.

In *Walk the Talk*, Harvey and Ventura[35] (2007) discuss the importance of five key principles of ethics for every professional; however, we feel that they aligned with ISLLC and are pertinent for school leadership—words to live by are just words unless you actually live by them; you are what you do; everything you do counts; the "golden rule" is still pure gold; and character is the key. The principles of character are commitment, honesty, accountability, respect, attitude, courage, trust, ethics and integrity, and responsibility. Students, teachers, and other staff members must view the leader as exhibiting these principles tied to decision making and so many aspects of the school.

In addition, several of these principles of character are essential in building positive school cultures. Phillips and Wagner[36] (2003) cite that one of the more fundamental principles of school culture is collegiality. Trust is a fundamental principle of collegiality where people respect each other, can be honest, and have positive attitudes. In standard 1 and standard 2, the importance of culture was discussed along with the role that the leader plays in "setting a tone for high expectations for teaching and learning." The leader must also set the tone for cultural expectations aligned with ethics. Furthermore, the leader has to model the principles. Most theorists will agree that trust is earned. Trust is earned through honesty and openness.

The Association of American Educators has established a code of ethics. The goals are to create learning environments so that all students fulfill their potentials, to have educators make conscientious efforts to exemplify standards, and to have educators accept responsibility that all children have a right to an education. There are four principles:

Principle I—Ethical conduct toward students
Principle II—Ethical conduct toward practices and performance
Principle III—Ethical conduct toward professional colleagues
Principle IV—Ethical conduct toward parents and community

## STANDARD 6

Standard 6 (The Political, Social, Economic, Legal, and Cultural Context of Learning) addresses understanding, responding to, and influencing the larger political, social, economic, legal, and cultural contexts.

School leaders must have knowledge of educational theory and be able to apply research methods to school. In addressing standard 3, we discussed the importance of school management with specific implications to teaching and learning—school leaders must also have knowledge of leadership theory, motivational theory, climate research, student achievement research, school law, and societal issues like poverty, in addition to cultural information about student populations. Principals need to demonstrate application of theories and relevant information to their specific schools.

Embedded in standard 6 is also the need for principals to understand and apply policies, laws, and regulations from federal, state, and local levels that impact schools. There are policies, laws, and regulations governing school management—in the state of Louisiana, schools must be open for a specified number of contact hours. There are policies, laws, and regulations governing both management and academics—specific subject areas are designated specific contact minutes by grade level. An additional important managerial function is aligned with the role of the school leader in finances. A great deal of specificity must be followed with purchases and accounting principles in schools that are ultimately the responsibility of leaders.

IDEAL is a federal legislation governing many principles of the education of special needs students. The educational services of special needs students are governed by individualized educational plans. Every student is also entitled to rights such as freedom of expression, privacy, due process, and for teachers to act "*in loco parentis*," which means that the teachers must act in the place of parents. In addition to student rights, principals must be knowledgeable and apply the rights of teachers. Generally, teachers have the right to freedom of expression, privacy, religious association, political association, due process/tenure, and academic freedom.

In standard 4, the importance of school and community relations programs was discussed. It is also important for principals to communicate with the school communities regarding trends and issues, in addition to policies, regulations, and laws. According to Holliday (1998),[37] educators communicate poorly. Communication abilities are also vital to leadership—communication is important to every standard—facilitating the vision of learning, the culture of teaching and learning, management of learning, relations with broader community to foster learning, integrity, fairness, and ethics in learning as well as the political, social, economic, legal, and cultural context of learning.

## CONCLUSION

The standards were discussed from the perspective of important knowledge, skills, and dispositions for principals; there are additional implications for school supervisors and school superintendents. As discussed in chapter 5, the responsibilities for school leaders in this era are intensifying as linked to the challenges of accountability. In chapter 7, the standards are discussed as aligned with SLLA.

## NOTES

1. About ISSLC (2003, February). Retrieved from www.umsl.edu/~mpea/Pages/About ISSLC/.

2. Hessel, H., & Holloway, J. (2001, September). School Leaders and Standards: A Vision for Leadership. Retrieved from www.icponline.org/feature_articles/f1401.htm.

3. Kowalski (2010).

4. Blankstein, A. (2010). *Failure Is Not an Option.* California: Corwin.
5. Fritz, R. (1996). *Corporate Tide: The Inescapable Laws of Organizational Structures.* San Franscisco: Verett-Koelher.
6. Conley, D. T., Dunlap, D. M., & Goldman, P. (1990). The Vision Thing and School Restructuring (OSSC Report 32), 1–8. Oregon: Eugene Oregon School Study Council.
7. Carr, A. (1995). Performance Technologists Preparation: The Role of Leadership Theory. *Performance Quarterly* 8: 50–74.
8. Kowalski, T. (2012). *Case Studies on Educational Administration.* 6th ed. Boston: Pearson.
9. Ubben, G., Hughes, L., & Norris, C. (2011). *The Principal: Creative Leadership for Excellence in Schools.* Boston: Pearson.
10. Kose, B. (2008, March). Developing a School Vision: Lessons from Nominated Transformative Principals. Paper presented at the annual meeting of the American Educational Research Association, University of Illinois.
11. Blankstein, A. (2010). *Failure Is Not an Option.* California: Corwin.
12. Kowalski, T. (2012). *Case Studies on Educational Administration.* Boston: Pearson.
13. Phillips, G., & Wagner, C. (2003). *School Culture Assessment: A Manual for Assessing and Transforming School-Classroom Culture.* Canada: Mitchell Press.
14. Ibid.
15. Ibid.
16. Louisiana Department of Education, Office of Quality Control, Division of Professional Development, Leadership Development. (2007). *Standards for School Principals.* Baton Rouge, LA.
17. Collins, J. (2001.) *Good to Great.* New York: HarperCollins.
18. Gray, D. (2009, January). A New Look at Instructional Leadership. *International Journal of Educational Leadership Preparation* 4(1).
19. Ubben, G., Hughes, L., & Norris, C. (2011). *The Principal: Creative Leadership for Excellence in Schools.* Boston: Pearson.
20. Connors, N. (2003). If You Don't Feed the Teachers, They Will Eat the Students. Nashville: Incentive.
21. Hoy, W., & Miskel, C. (2008). *Educational Administration: Theory, Research, and Practice.* 8th ed. New York: McGraw-Hill.
22. 22. Ibid.
23. Zepeda, S. (2003). *Instructional Supervision: Applying Tools and Concepts.* New York: Eye on Education.
24. Chicago Public Schools. Five Fundamentals for School Success.
25. Hoy, W., & Miskel, C. (2008). *Educational Administration: Theory, Research, and Practice.* 8th ed. New York: McGraw-Hill.
26. Ibid.
27. Freiberg, H., Prokosch, N., Treister, E., & Stein, T. (1990).Turning Around Five At-Risk Elementary Schools. *School Effectiveness & School Improvement* 1: 5–25.
28. Hoy, W., & Miskel, C. (2008). *Educational Administration; Theory, Research, and Practice.* 8th ed. New York: McGraw-Hill.
29. Hoy, W., & Miskel, C. (2008). *Educational Administration: Theory, Research, and Practice.* 8th ed. New York: McGraw-Hill.
30. Henderson, A., & Berla, N. (1994). *The Family Is Critical to Student Achievement.* Washington, DC: National Center for Law and Education.
31. Epstein, J., Sanders, M., Simon, B., Salinas, K., Jansom, N., & Van Voorhis, F. (2002). *School, Family, and Community Partnerships: Your Handbook for Action.* California: Corwin.
32. Ibid.
33. Martin, R. (1995). *The Schoolhome: Rethinking Schools for Changing Families.* Cambridge, MA: Harvard University Press.
34. Jones, L., & Kennedy, E. (2008). *Passing the Leadership Test: A Study Guide for the School Leaders Licensure Examination.* Lanham, MD: Rowman & Littlefield.
35. Harvey, E., &Ventura, S. (2007). *Walk the Talk.* Texas: Walk The Talk Company.
36. Phillips, G., & Wagner, C. (2003). *School Culture Assessment.* Canada: Mitchell Press.

37. Holliday, A. (1988, 2nd Quarter). "In Search of an Answer. What Is School Public Relations?" *Journal of Education Public Relations*: 12.

# Chapter Seven

# Standards Linked to Examination

## NATURE OF THE TEST

As previously addressed, the ISLCC standards were revised in 2008 but initially developed through the leadership of the Council of Chief State School Officers and several states and professional organizations. Several states led the initiative in 1999 to take the standards further by requiring principals to pass a six-hour performance examination—the School Leader Licensure Assessment. The initial test was composed of ten brief scenarios (vignettes) that candidates were to address. The test has been redesigned several times.

The School Leaders Licensure Assessment 2009 version is a one-hundred-item multiple-choice test (section I) with a seven-item constructed-responses section (section II). The time allotted for section I is two hours and twenty minutes; the time allotted for section II is one hour and forty minutes. For the constructed responses, test takers are required to "analyze situations and data, to propose appropriate courses of action, and to provide rationales for their proposals."[1] For section II, the focus is standard 1—Vision and Goals; standard 2—Teaching and Learning; and standard 6—The Educational System. Sample constructed-response items will be provided in this chapter. In addition, in chapter 8 case studies are presented that address all of the standards; therefore, they are also good items for purposes of review.

Table 7.1, from ETS, depicts the number of questions as aligned with content categories; the content categories are the standards.

## SCORING

The scoring of the multiple-choice questions is obvious; correct or incorrect responses from four choices. For the constructed responses, in the previous section of this chapter the ETS web source is cited as being linked to the expectations of the responses and the foci (standard 1, standard 2, standard 6.) The following is a sample scoring guide as linked to standard 1—Vision and Goals. The scores range from 0 to 3.

### Sample Scoring for Vision and Goals

A response that receives a score of 3 demonstrates a thorough understanding of how to develop shared commitments and responsibilities among staff and the community for carrying out the vision and goals and/or communicating the vision and goals in ways that facilitate key stakeholders' ability to understand, support, and act upon the vision and goals.

A typical response in this category:

- demonstrates strong knowledge of principles of communication and group processes (building consensus, motivating, and team building);
- demonstrates strong knowledge of implementation and/or change strategies;
- provides a clear and specific response to the question asked;
- prioritizes, outlines, or organizes steps or actions in a logical and insightful manner; and

| Content Categories | Approximate Number of Questions | Approximate Percentage of Examination |
|---|---|---|
| *Section 1* | | |
| Vision and Goals | 18 | 12 |
| Teaching and Learning | 25 | 18 |
| Managing Organizational Systems and Safety | 15 | 10 |
| Collaborating with Key Stakeholders | 21 | 15 |
| Ethics and Integrity | 21 | 15 |
| *Section II* | | |
| The Education System | 2 | 10 |
| Vision and Goals (Constructed Response) | 2 | 8 |
| Teaching and Learning (Constructed Response) | 3 | 12 |

Table 7.1. ETS School Leaders Licensure Assessment 1011

- provides logical and reasonable rationales for answers when requested.

A response that receives a score of 2 demonstrates a basic/general understanding of how to develop shared commitments and responsibilities among staff and the community for carrying out the vision and goals and/or communicating the vision and goals in ways that facilitate key stakeholders' ability to understand, support, and act upon the vision and goals.

A typical response in this category:

- demonstrates adequate knowledge of principles of communication and group processes (building consensus, motivating, and team building);
- demonstrates adequate knowledge of implementation and/or change strategies;
- provides an appropriate response to the question asked;
- prioritizes, outlines, or organizes steps or actions in an orderly manner; and
- provides acceptable rationales for answers when requested.

A response that receives a score of 1 demonstrates a limited understanding of how to develop shared commitments and responsibilities among staff and the community for carrying out the vision and goals and/or communicating the vision and goals in ways that facilitate key stakeholders' ability to understand, support, and act upon the vision and goals.

A typical response in this category reveals one or more of the following weaknesses:

- demonstrates limited knowledge of principles of communication and group processes (building consensus, motivating, and team building);
- demonstrates limited knowledge of implementation and/or change strategies;
- provides an uneven or unclear response to the question asked;
- prioritizes, outlines, or organizes steps or actions unclearly or with gaps in logic; and
- provides partial or limited rationales for answers when requested.

A response that receives a score of 0 demonstrates little or no understanding of how to develop shared commitments and responsibilities among staff and the community for carrying out the vision and goals and/or communicating the vision and goals in ways that facilitate key stakeholders' ability to understand, support, and act upon the vision and goals.

A typical response in this category reveals one or more of the following weaknesses:

- demonstrates weak or no knowledge of principles of communication and group processes (building consensus, motivating, and team building);
- demonstrates weak or no knowledge of implementation and/or change strategies;
- provides a vague or inappropriate answer to the question;
- fails to prioritize, outline, or organize steps or actions or does so illogically;
- provides a weak, inappropriate, or illogical rationale or does not provide a rationale when one is requested; and
- no credit is given for a blank or off-topic response.

## Sample Constructed Responses

*Sample Test Question for Implementing Vision and Goals (from ETS's Guide)*

*The sample question that follows illustrates the kind of question in the test. It is not, however, representative of the entire scope of the test in either content or difficulty. Answers with explanations follow the question.* A new principal in a suburban school district with six elementary schools has been asked to support the continuing implementation of a nontraditional math program at her school. The program was implemented district-wide three years ago amid considerable concern from parents and staff. Frequent evaluation of the program has shown that students' conceptual understanding is exceptional, but their computation performance varies from year to year and consistently falls below their conceptual understanding. While significant concerns still linger among parents and staff, parent satisfaction has increased by 20 percent in the last year and dissatisfaction has declined by one third. The site evaluation team has established several recommendations, including improving communication with parents and providing professional development for teachers.

*Question*

Identify and describe at least three steps the principal can take to gain further support for the program and decrease the dissatisfaction levels.

*Sample 1: Score 3*

As the new principal, there are several steps that I would take to gain further support and decrease the level of dissatisfaction with the new math program. First, I would establish monthly math nights. These events would allow parents to attend with their children and participate together in a lesson presented by the teacher. The parents would get a better understanding of the math program and learn how they can help their children at home.

I would also establish a math homework hotline. This hotline would be staffed by teachers each evening and would be a resource for both students and parents to call with questions and assistance. Besides helping with a particular assignment, this would also be a great way to lessen parents' frustrations with the new program and as a result decrease dissatisfaction. Another step would be to survey staff to see whether they need additional professional development. After the survey results were analyzed, there are many types of professional development that I would use, such as mentors, attending conferences, bringing in outside resources, and visiting nearby schools that have successfully implemented the same math program.

Finally, I would require teachers to increase communication with parents. This could be done by having the teacher write a "math gram" to parents at the beginning of each new unit. The newsletter would explain the concepts of the new unit and give parents ideas on how to do fun math things at home.

## Comments on Sample 1: Score 3

This response demonstrates the complexity of the situation and the need to bring key stakeholders on board for the program to ultimately succeed. It begins by acknowledging that the problem will take multiple steps to solve and that the most pressing need is to increase overall familiarity with and support for the program. The principal seeks to develop shared commitments and responsibilities by establishing math nights and a math homework hot-line. These two actions will bring key stakeholders (parents, teachers, and students) together in ways that will foster greater acceptance of the math program. To increase support for the program among staff, the principal recommends using a professional development survey and identifies several activities that would increase teacher knowledge of the new math program. Finally, the principal will use teachers to communicate the direction of the math program with parents by implementing a regular newsletter. Stakeholder-to-stakeholder communication will strengthen support for the math program. Holistically, the response is clear and organized, and the answers given are acceptable and well developed. Overall, this response demonstrates a thorough understanding of how to increase support for a program by developing shared commitment among stakeholders.

## Sample Multiple Choice

### Sample Test Questions

*The sample questions that follow illustrate the kinds of questions in the test. They are not, however, representative of the entire scope of the test in either content or difficulty. Answers with explanations follow the questions.*

Directions: Each of the questions or statements below is followed by four suggested answers or completions. Select the one that is best in each case. Questions 1–3 are based on the following scenario:

A principal has been appointed to an elementary school in which the scores on the fourth-grade state language-arts tests have been decreasing each year for the past three years. The weakest area is writing. With a goal of improving writing instruction, the principal and the fourth-grade teachers decide to set aside time to examine and discuss student writing samples as a group.

1. Each teacher brings copies of student writing samples to share with the group. Which of the following actions should the teachers take first to improve instruction?

(A) Conducting an analytical review of all papers to assign scores
(B) Reviewing all papers to identify common areas of weakness
(C) Targeting students in need of remediation based on the samples provided
(D) Identifying benchmark-quality samples to use as exemplars for next year's instruction

2. Over the course of several weeks, the principal observes each of the fourth-grade teachers. In light of the concern about improving students' scores on language-arts assessments, the principal's primary concern should be whether the teachers

(A) align their lesson objectives with their teaching strategies and materials
(B) match their lesson plans with the lessons actually taught
(C) include teaching strategies that meet the needs of diverse learners
(D) match their lesson objectives with the fourth-grade language-arts standards

3. Which of the following two pieces of information would be most relevant for the principal to use to help the teachers determine strategies for improving fourth-grade students' achievement in language arts?

(A) the school's vision statement and student demographic information
(B) the language-arts block schedule for the fourth-grade classrooms and the reading levels of each fourth-grade student
(C) the language-arts standards for fourth-grade students and disaggregated standardized test data
(D) the educational background and years of experience of the fourth-grade teachers

4. Recommended practice suggests which of the following should be involved in the decision-making process concerning curriculum?

I. Curriculum experts
II. Boards of education
III. Professional staff
IV. Students

(A) I and III only
(B) II and III only
(C) III and IV only
(D) I, II, and III only

5. Which of the following is the most crucial question to consider in using community resources in the classroom?

(A) Can the resources be used by several groups at the same time?
(B) Have such resources been overused?
(C) Do the resources meet the needs of the program?
(D) What time limits have been established for the use of the resources?

6. A group of high-school English teachers have approached the newly appointed department chair with concerns about the existing curriculum. The teachers explain that the curriculum has not been revised in nearly ten years and is out of date. In response to the teachers' concerns, the department chair should first

(A) review the research on exemplary high-school English programs
(B) convene a meeting with the parents, superintendent, and board of education to gather their input
(C) collaborate with the teachers to examine the alignment between the existing curriculum and state standards
(D) immediately begin to analyze the curriculum and observe classroom instruction

7. According to due process, teachers are entitled to

(A) the presence of a defense counsel at any hearing and the right to refuse to testify
(B) adequate notice of the charges against them and a hearing in which they have the opportunity to defend themselves against those charges
(C) an appeal of an adverse decision and exemption from disciplinary action while the appeal is being decided
(D) a cross-examination of an adverse witness and the control of conditions under which such examination takes place

8. Of the following evaluation methods, which would provide the most valid indication of the success of a course of study in meeting its instructional goals?

(A) compiling results of a survey of the students' opinions of the course

(B) reviewing anecdotal records that describe students' interpersonal growth during the course

(C) reviewing data that indicate the degree of students' mastery of course objectives

(D) surveying parents about the students' transfer of concepts learned in the course

9. The newly appointed principal of an elementary school is concerned about the performance of the fourth grade on the state standardized tests for mathematics. Which of the following should be the principal's initial step in developing a plan to improve students' scores?

(A) Hire a staff developer to teach staff innovative approaches to mathematics instruction

(B) Collect information about the instructional methods, materials, and assessments currently in use

(C) Conduct a curriculum audit of the mathematics program at all grade levels

(D) Administer another assessment to identify specific areas of weakness in students' performance

10. A department chair is concerned about a few students in the advanced-level biology class who have received barely passing or failing grades on their first-marking-period report cards while their classmates have performed well. Which of the following areas of investigation is likely to provide the most valuable information for explaining the weak performance of some students?

(A) teacher records of tests grades, homework assignments, and class participation

(B) National Science Education content standards for the appropriate grade level

(C) the currency and appropriateness of the instructional materials in the course

(D) admission standards for the advanced-level science classes

*Answers*

*1.* This question focuses on the school leader's understanding of how to provide instruction that meets the standards of rigor measured by standardized assessment. Choices (A) and (D) describe steps in the process, but neither would be the initial step. Choice (C) may serve to address weaknesses in a specific group but does little to improve overall writing instruction.

Identifying specific areas of weakness will help teachers focus instruction and assessment on those areas most likely to be adversely affecting students' scores. Therefore, the correct answer is (B).

*2.* This question tests the school leader's knowledge of factors that affect standardized test results. Choices (A), (B), and (C) are all sound practices but do not address the primary focus of the question. The principal needs to verify whether there is an alignment between lesson objectives and state standards, which serves as the basis of state standardized tests. Therefore, the correct answer is (D).

*3.* This question tests the school leader's knowledge of information necessary to make instructional decisions. For the purpose of determining strategies to improve fourth-grade students' achievement, it is important to know the standards and test data. The standards serve as the foundation for the curriculum and knowing what to teach. Disaggregated test data would clarify both the areas that have been addressed and the areas that need to be targeted. Therefore, the correct answer is (C).

*4.* Curriculum experts, boards of education, and school professional staff should all be part of the decision-making process concerning curriculum matters. Choice (D) includes all three groups and is the correct answer.

*5.* This question asks a school leader to determine which of many considerations is most important when community resources are integrated into classroom instruction. Choices (A), (B), and (D) become considerations only after it has been determined that the resources support the needs of the program. Therefore, the correct answer is (C).

*6.* This question tests the school leader's knowledge of how state standards are used to measure the quality and appropriateness of a curriculum. Choices (A) and (B) are actions that may be taken during the course of curriculum revision but would not be the initial step. Choice (D) would provide unreliable information because teachers who have already acknowledged the inappropriateness of the current written curriculum would most likely not be following it consistently. Involving the teachers in the examination of the curriculum as measured against benchmarks would provide the most useful information for moving the curriculum process forward; therefore, the correct answer is (C).

*7.* This question tests the school leader's knowledge of the basic due process protections afforded to school personnel. Although individual teacher contracts, local school board policies, or collective bargaining agreements may offer the additional protections described in choices (A), (C), and (D), only those described in choice (B) are guaranteed to all personnel under the Constitution and key court rulings. Therefore, (B) is the correct answer.

*8.* This question tests the school leader's understanding of how to select the most accurate method for evaluating the effectiveness of a course of study in meeting its learning objectives. Choices (A), (B), and (D) will provide information on the effectiveness of a course in meeting other objectives. However, only choice (C) provides evaluative information directly related to students' understanding of the knowledge and skills as described in the course's instructional goals. Therefore, the correct answer is (C).

*9.* This question tests the school leader's understanding of the steps in the process of addressing an educational problem. Choices (A) and (C) are valid actions but would occur later in the process. Choice (D) is unnecessary because information on areas of weakness will have been provided in the scoring data of the state assessment. Gaining a sense of the overall fourth-grade mathematics program as it currently exists will most likely result in the identification of specific areas needing improvement. Therefore, the correct answer is (B).

*10.* This question tests the school leader's ability to select the appropriate data for providing specific educational information. Looking at teacher records will offer evidence of students' weak performance but not an explanation. Examining choices (B) and (C) might indicate inconsistencies that would likely affect the performance of all the students, not just a few. When students experience difficulty in a class from the onset, one reasonable explanation can be that the criteria used for their placement are not appropriate. Therefore, the correct answer is (D).

As presented in table 7.1, ETS School Leaders Licensure Assessment 1011 (at the beginning of the chapter), the multiple-choice items are aligned with ISLCC standard 1, Vision and Goals; standard 2, Teaching and Learning; standard 3, Managing Organizational Systems and Safety; standard 4, Collaborating with Stakeholders; and standard 5, Ethics and Integrity. The following are concepts that are linked to the standards that candidates should review in alignment with the previously cited standards discussed in chapter 6, for both the multiple-choice and constructive-response items:

- curriculum and instruction;
- lesson planning;
- data analyses;
- professional development;
- school improvement planning;
- school culture and climate;
- decision making;
- leadership theory;
- motivational theories;
- communication;
- budgeting principles;
- facilities planning;
- school and community relations;
- parental involvement; and

- legal and policy issues (teacher and student rights, zero tolerance, religion and public schools, separation of church and state, special-needs students and IEPs, behavioral policies, teacher tenure, teacher autonomy).

The following scenarios were included in Version 1 of *Passing the Leadership Test* and are helpful in assisting candidates in preparing holistically with respect to the application of the standards. These two scenarios first appeared in R. L. Green (2009), *Practicing the Art of Leadership*, third edition.

## SCENARIO 1: THE NEW PRINCIPAL AT FROST

This scenario allows candidates to apply standards 1, 2, 3, and 4 of ISLCC:

Standard 1 (The Vision of Learning), facilitating the development, articulation, implementation, and stewardship of a vision of learning that is shared and supported by all stakeholders.

Standard 2 (The Culture of Teaching and Learning), advocating, nurturing, and sustaining a school culture and instructional program conducive to student learning and staff professional growth.

Standard 3 (Management of Learning), ensuring management of the organization, operation, and resources for a safe, efficient, and effective learning environment.

Standard 4 (Relations with Broader Community to Foster Learning), collaborating with faculty and community members, responding to diverse community interests and needs, and mobilizing community resources.

### The New Principal at Frost

Frost Elementary School, with a population of 1,100 students, pre-K–6, is located in the inner city of a larger southern metropolitan area. The ethnic/socioeconomic makeup of the school is African American and poor. The faculty composition is 45 percent Caucasian and 55 percent African American. Although the school district has been desegregated for a number of years, Frost's enrollment remains totally African American.

Scores on achievement tests, which are used to measure student progress and serve as a means of comparison with students in other parts of the city and state, are at an all-time low. They have been some of the lowest scores in the district for a number of years. Mr. Shaw, who served as principal of the school for fifteen years, was considered by most faculty members to be an individual who loved children and had their best interests at heart. He was always in the community conveying to parents his interest in the children, the school, and the community. Mr. Shaw was quite knowledgeable and worked diligently with the faculty to enhance the school's instructional program. However, in spite of his efforts, achievement scores remained low and incidents of discipline high. During the last five years of his tenure, the average daily attendance of students fluctuated between 84 percent and 86 percent. Nevertheless, his traditional instructional program was highly supported by faculty and students and staff. In addition, the school was several thousand dollars in debt, and fund-raising was virtually nonexistent.

With the appointment of the new superintendent and a push for educational reform and restructuring, Mr. Shaw retired, and Dr. Sterling was appointed principal. Upon her appointment, she received directions to improve student achievement at Frost, using some form of site-based management. During the first week of her assignment, she sent the following memorandum to the staff:

MEMORANDUM to Faculty & Staff:
August 21, 2007

I would like to request volunteers to serve on a task force to develop a plan of action to bring about improvements in the instructional program here at Frost. One of the responsibilities of the task force will be to survey the entire faculty and staff for the purpose of ascertaining their ideals, suggestions, and recommendations for program improvements. The work of the task force will be very time consuming; however, the results should propel us into the twenty-first century and beyond.

Please notify my secretary by September 1, 2007, if you are available to serve. Thank you for your cooperation in this matter.

On September 1, Dr. Sterling asked her secretary for the list of volunteers; there were no responses. The word of the grapevine was, "The new principal has considerable work in mind for the faculty, and the faculty is already totally consumed with maintaining discipline."

## Selecting the Task Force

Having received no volunteers, the principal invited (selected) one teacher from each grade level to serve on the task force. The individuals selected were not thrilled about being drafted; however, they accepted the principal's invitation and attended the first meeting on September 5, 2007. All subsequent meetings were held once a week (between Principal Sterling and the task force) until the plan was ready for partial implementation on October 2, 2007.

## Developing the Plan

The task force met for approximately forty hours developing the plan. Having read Leo Bradley's (1993) *Total Quality Management for Schools*, the principal introduced the task force to the affinity, fishbone, and Pareto designs. (The reader will find it beneficial to read Bradley's *Total Quality Management for Schools* to fully understand the techniques, which are excellent approaches to assessing the prevailing conditions for a school.)

The faculty at Frost used the affinity diagram to brainstorm and define the issues that needed to be addressed. The affinity diagram allowed the principal to organize output from the brainstorming session of the task force. Using this design, all of the information could be consolidated. The fishbone diagram (cause and effect) was used to get an overall picture of how to move from current reality to the established goals. Using this design, elements that may have been contributing to the problem and their cause-and-effect relationships could be identified. The Pareto diagram (a simple bar chart) was utilized to identify the pros and cons of various challenging school issues (separating major problems from trivial ones) and to ensure that the programs selected for implementation would be effective. Reports were provided to the faculty and staff, who, in turn, provided feedback to the task force on their work. Of the issues identified, the most pressing was student discipline. Thus, the task force made the recommendations to the principal that improving school-wide discipline should be the first issue addressed. Principal Sterling accepted the recommendation, and improving student behavior school-wide became the order of the day.

## Implementing the Plan

Realizing that faculty would need professional development to effectively implement new programs in the area of discipline, Principal Sterling again turned to the task force for an assessment of the faculty's professional development program needs. By a large majority, the faculty voted to be trained in various methods of assertive discipline, discipline with dignity, and discipline techniques for today's children. In addition, the faculty requested that Principal Sterling formally develop a school-wide discipline plan and schedule workshops during faculty meetings so that teachers could begin to implement various techniques in their classrooms. They also requested that Dr. Sterling actively recruit male teachers to provide students with male role models. In concluding their work, the task force clearly stated, "For the new programs to be successful, it will be necessary for all faculty and staff to be involved. There can be no exceptions."

In subsequent meetings with the task force, a decision was reached to open the lines of communication between the home and school so that parents would not feel isolated from the process. Principal Sterling announced an open-door policy and instituted school conferences to inform parents about appropriate and inappropriate behaviors. Communication to homes included phone calls, notes from teachers, and monthly informational calendars. An automated phone system was installed, and a website was created to keep parents informed of all school activities and events.

## Results of the Plan

During the first year, discipline was hard and fast; eighty out-of-school suspensions were issued to students. Parents were extremely upset—they never had this problem with the previous principal. However, the administration, faculty, and staff held firm. Parent workshops were conducted on parenting skills and the fair, firm, and consistent policies used by the administration, faculty, and staff. The faculty was able to focus on the instructional program.

After improvement in discipline began to occur, Principal Sterling turned to the second item on the list generated by the faculty: "curriculum, instruction, and evaluation." Again, she asked for individuals to serve on a committee, and this time the responses were quite different; sixteen individuals volunteered to serve. In her businesslike manner, Principal Sterling accepted all sixteen, and the committee went to work. After three weeks of discussion, the committee determined that the school had to change and change drastically. Student regression (failure to retain information from the previous year) over the summer nullified any achievement gains the students had made the previous year. Year-round education was determined to be the educational course for the school to pursue.

## Remaining on the Fast Track

To continue to make improvements at Frost, subcommittees were formed for various initiatives, frequent fund-raising events were held, teachers were in the community visiting with parents, and instructional planning meetings were continual. With the planning and implementation of year-round education, Frost became the talk of the educational community. Professors from the local university took an interest in the school and often asked to be allowed to help implement programs. Visitors from other schools in the city, state, and other states in the nation frequently visited the school, and Principal Sterling received and accepted invitations to participate in a variety of local, state, and national conferences. At the end of Principal Sterling's fourth year, discipline had improved. The year-round school concept had been implemented, and most of the faculty members were supporting the site-based management concept. However, teacher turnover was about 10 percent. Some of the turnover appeared to be initiated by the principal, and some was teacher initiated.

## Discussion on Standards

There are so many reflective questions that could be asked to address the ISLLC standards 1, 2, 3, and 4. Obvious concepts embedded in the scenario include Sterling's vision (standard 1), the importance of curriculum (standard 2), the need for school management to be prevalent (standard 3), and the involvement of the community in various stages of the school improvement (standard 4).

To address any reflective questions linked to this scenario, candidates must address all standards previously alluded to. In her use of standard 1, Sterling uses strategic planning and team and consensus building to gain support from the staff. Dr. Sterling does not mention school improvement frequently; however, it is her mission to improve the entire climate of the school. She also applies the motivational theories in getting staff input through the implementation of what is recommended by the staff. Standard 2 is viable as the staff development is provided to support a school-wide change.

The management skills (standard 3) exemplified by Dr. Sterling are critical in supporting school-wide change. The concepts recommended by the teachers are definitely implemented and supported by Sterling. Initially, there is some resistance from the community, linked to the increase in suspension levels. However, Sterling acknowledges the functions of the community by establishing and maintaining an open-door policy (standard 4).

Candidates should also include in discussion to Scenario 1 the functions of standards 1, 2, 3, and 4 cited by ISLLC.

## SCENARIO 2: RETAINING THE STUDENT RECOGNITION PROGRAM

Standard 5: An education leader promotes the success of every student by acting with integrity, fairness, and in an ethical manner.

Standard 6: An education leader promotes the success of every student by understanding, responding to, and influencing the political, social, economic, legal, and cultural context.

Overfield High School is a large 9–12 urban high school with a student population of three thousand. Over the past six years, the school has experienced an increase in discipline problems and a decline in student achievement and attendance. At least two students have been expelled for having weapons on campus.

In an attempt to change this trend, the principal and staff made a commitment to implement a student-recognition program. The program has been in operation for four years. During the first two years of the program, there was a decline in discipline problems, and the faculty had been quite different. Discipline problems are now increasing, attendance has fallen by two percentage points, and Principal Jones has noticed signs of waning faculty enthusiasm for the program. In fact, the original energetic and enthusiastic core of fifteen teachers who conceptualized the program and influenced the faculty and student body to adopt it has now dwindled to a group of five overworked individuals. Principal Jones realized that something had to be done or the program would fall apart, and all the original gains would be lost. Therefore, early in the spring, he scheduled a series of meetings to review the programs.

During the spring review, teachers voiced concerns that the students were losing their excitement about the rewards associated with the program. The faculty also reported instances where they had heard students complain about boredom—too much time sitting still, the "same old prizes," and too-stiff attendance guidelines. Relative to their involvement, the faculty expressed concerns regarding the program guidelines. On the positive side, the faculty reported that students expressed enjoyment of the use of their field trips, tickets for special events, dances, and food as "prizes." At the conclusion of the review, it was decided that the student recognition program was a good program that simply needed to be revitalized.

Once the faculty recognized the areas of the program they needed to revise, they spent hours in five different meetings, generating and evaluating ideas and identifying possible changes to the program. After the fifth meeting, Principal Jones looked at his exhausted faculty and said to them, "You have done an excellent job. I will take all of your suggestions, compile them, and send you a copy of the compilation during June for review. We will meet in late August to discuss and finalize the program for the next school year."

The faculty appeared very energized, and everyone left school feeling a sense of accomplishment and voiced satisfaction with the outlook for the next school year.

## Discussion on Standards

Obvious concepts embedded in scenario 2 include the need for the school leader to assess the programs of the school as linked to effectiveness of the school, to utilize effective decision making linked to diversity and ethical principles, to improve the communication, and to account for input of all stakeholders regarding the vision of the school.

To address questions and reflection of the SLLA pertinent to standards 5 and 6, the obvious choices include candidates discussing the functions of both of the standards (cited in chapter 6).

### SCHOOL SUPERINTENDENT ASSESSMENT (1020)

According to ETS,[2] the School Superintendent Assessment (1020) is a three-hour assessment; the test design targets components required for a school superintendent as aligned with the ISLLC standards. It is a three-hour assessment with three testing modules—Evaluation of Actions (module I); Synthesis of Information and Problem Solving (module II); and Analysis of Information and Decision Making (module III).

For module I, there are five vignettes. Candidates are required to answer questions regarding group processes, student learning, resources and operations, and content identified in job analyses. In module II, candidates are required to respond to short scenarios. The content covered includes teaching and learning interrelated with boards of education and community involvement. For module III, scenarios are presented with content similar to module II. The difference in module III is that candidates are also given documents to analyze. The kinds of documents include assessment data, components of school or district improvement plans, budget information, resource allocation documents, and curriculum information.

According to www.ets.org/Media/Tests/SLS/pdf/1020.pdf, the following are the types of questions that are included in module III:

- What is an important issue in the data presented in this document?
- What other information would you need to assess the information presented in the document?
- Where would you get such information?
- What important patterns do you observe in the data presented in the document?
- What steps would you take with your staff to address the issues raised by the data presented in the document?
- How would you present the information contained in this document to parents, community organizations, staff, and others?

## Module 1: Evaluation of Actions

All five exercises in the Evaluation of Actions module are scored on a three-point scale, with 2 the highest possible score and 0 the lowest.

*Sample Exercise*

Currently there are two elementary schools in a district. A new K–5 elementary school is opening in the fall. It will be necessary to determine which students will attend each of the three schools, necessitating the formation of new boundary lines.

Identify and describe at least three critical factors the superintendent should include in a recommendation to the board of education about the new boundary lines.

*Relevant ISLLC Standards*

Standards 3 and 5

*General Scoring Guide*

The following general scoring guide is used to score all responses in the Evaluation of Actions module.

*Score: 2.* A score of 2 presents a reasoned response based on a clear understanding and application of the underlying standards.

A typical response in this category

- demonstrates a clear understanding of the standards applicable to the vignette;
- applies the appropriate standards in a manner that is consistent with the intent and spirit of the standards;
- provides a clear and specific answer to the question asked; and
- provides a logical and reasonable rationale for answers when requested.

*Score: 1.* A score of 1 presents a response based on a general understanding and application of the underlying standards but may also be uneven in its presentation.

A typical response in this category:

- demonstrates a general understanding of the standards applicable to the vignette;
- applies the standards in a manner that is supportive of the intent and spirit of the standards;
- provides a general or uneven answer to the question; and
- provides an acceptable rationale for answers when requested.

*Score: 0.* A score of 0 may demonstrate some competence in responding to the question but is clearly limited or flawed.

A typical response in this category:

- demonstrates a weak understanding of the standards applicable to the vignette;
- does not apply appropriate standards or applies standards in opposition to the intent and spirit of the standard;
- provides a vague or inappropriate answer to the question; and
- provides a weak, inappropriate, or illogical rationale or does not provide a rationale when one is requested.

## Module II: Synthesis of Information and Problem Solving

The exercise (case) in the Synthesis of Information and Problem Solving module is scored on a four-point scale, with 3 the highest possible score and 0 the lowest. The responses to the four questions within the exercise are treated as a single response for scoring purposes, so only one score is assigned to the case.

*Sample Exercise*

In this module of assessment, use the scenario and documents provided on the following pages as the basis for answering questions.

## SCENARIO

The superintendent of the Greenwood Elementary School District has the responsibility for aligning the district's elementary curriculum with state standards in the language arts and mathematics areas. The goal is to ensure that students are proficient as measured by state assessments. The Greenwood district has a history of being progressive and forward thinking in terms of education in general and curriculum offerings in particular. A spirit of staff and community involvement and cooperation typifies the district's curriculum development initiatives.

The state has recently adopted new core curriculum standards in language arts literacy and mathematics. The new standards, a response to public outrage over declining student achievement in language arts and mathematics, mandate intensified programs, both in breadth and depth of coverage of concepts and skills. Many stakeholders, however, are resistant to the newly mandated curriculum standards as an infringement on "local control" and the possibility that "prized" programs and services may be eliminated.

## DOCUMENTS

The following documents are included:

- Letter to the commissioner of education from the president of the school board of education
- Letter to the president of the school board of education from the commissioner of education
- Article from the *Greenwood Daily News*
- Memo to the superintendent from the Greenwood Teachers Organization
- Memo to the superintendent from the director of curriculum and instruction of GESD

## QUESTIONS

The five documents that follow all relate to the situation described briefly above. Read all the documents carefully, and then respond to each of the following questions:

Based on your understanding of teaching and learning, as well as larger educational issues, what should be the superintendent's initial steps in enlisting the critical support and involvement of the board of education in the alignment of the district's curricula with these state curriculum standards? Explain why each of these steps is important.

What specific topics relative to the implementation of the state mandate should the superintendent place on the agenda for the Superintendent's Council and review with the board of education? Explain why each topic is important.

Describe essential elements of a plan for reporting to the board of education and to the public the progress being made toward implementation of the state mandate.

Identify specific groups of stakeholders who have responsibilities and needs in regard to the implementation of the state mandate. For each group, explain the impact of the mandate.

# DOCUMENT 1

Greenwood Elementary School
Board of Education
"We Honor All of Our Children"

April 2

To the Office of the State Commissioner of Education

Dear Commissioner:
On behalf of the Greenwood Elementary School District, I am writing to express concerns that we have with recent curriculum mandates of the state Department of Education.

Greenwood is a district with five elementary schools. We have major concerns about the mandated fourth-grade curriculum alignment requirements in the areas of language arts literacy and mathematics. In both areas, significant additions have been made to an already demanding curriculum. These additions present major problems for our district, as we suspect they do for many comparable districts.

Our district has a long history of considerable academic success as evidenced on our own standardized test scores as well as teacher-made assessments. Additionally, we provide our students multiple opportunities to experience a curriculum in the fine arts and many other areas. It is our position that the recently adopted curriculum mandate will harm, rather than benefit, the academic performance and growth of our students.

We request that you send us the proper forms by which we can request exemption from the recent curriculum mandates. If an exemption is not possible, we request a delay of implementation for at least three years. This delay will allow our teachers to prepare adequately for the new curriculum and allow time for the district to negotiate a new teachers' contract that takes into consideration the lengthened school day and altered teaching requirements of the new mandates.
Sincerely,
President, Greenwood Elementary School board of Education

# DOCUMENT 2

Office of the Commissioner of Education
State Department of Education

May 5

President, Greenwood Elementary School board of Education

Dear School Board President:

Thank you for sharing your concerns about the state-mandated curriculum alignment requirements for the state's elementary students. By law, there can be no exemptions and no postponements in the implementation of these requirements.

These alignment mandates are based on educational research and best practices investigated by the Division of Curriculum and instruction of the state Department of Education. The implementation of these alignment standards will enable all students to master more challenging communication and computational skills. This increased mastery will enable all students to enhance their potential for success in subsequent years of schooling and their ultimate entry to greater society. Increasing standards for all students in the state should not preclude your district from offering additional experiences such as the ones you mentioned in the fine arts.

Sincerely,
Commissioner of Education

# DOCUMENT 3

Greenwood Daily News

Parents Fear State Standards Will Cause Elimination of Special Programs for Gifted and Talented Students
May 10

Parents at the Greenwood Elementary District Board of Education meeting last night expressed strong concerns about the future of the district's programs for gifted and talented children, particularly in the fine arts. A recent presentation by the district's director of curriculum included recommendations for reducing time allocated to highly regarded programs, "in order to provide additional time for instruction required to meet the state's newly mandated curriculum standards in language arts literacy and mathematics."

"We fought so hard to get these special programs for our children into the curriculum. This seems like a huge step backwards. We are disappointed and angry," said a parent of three children in the district.

The meeting was very heated as times. The board president said, "We feel caught in a no-win situation. We must be sure that our students can perform well on the state's assessments. We don't know where to find the time to fit all these things in the school day. After all, these are very young children and we can't keep them here until late at night."

The board promised to continue to address this issue in the coming months.

# DOCUMENT 4

Greenwood Teacher's Organization
MEMORANDUM

TO: Superintendent, Greenwood Elementary School District
FROM: Greenwood Teacher's Organization
DATE: May 13
RE: Contract

We are writing to make to make official the concerns we have expressed in recent conversations with you about the necessity of reopening negotiations for the teaching contract effective July 1 of this year. We believe that the recently concluded negotiations resulted in a fair and equitable contract, and we appreciate the spirit of cooperation and professionalism of all concerned in the negotiations. However, as we have discussed, the refusal of the state to grant a waiver or a delay in the implementation of the new state curriculum standards clearly means that there will be a longer school day and teachers will have more demanding teaching responsibilities. Both of these provisions have been deemed necessary by the district in order to meet the state mandate and continue to offer the rich program of which our district is justly proud.

Both of these factors clearly require a modification in the contract. We are aware that the budget-building process for next year is complete. However, in view of the drastically changed teaching demands on the district's teachers, that process must be reopened and necessary funds identified to compensate teachers for their increased work load. We would like to meet with you at your earliest convenience to establish timelines and priorities for renegotiating the contract effective July 1.

# DOCUMENT 5

Office of the Director of Curriculum and Instruction
Greenwood Elementary School District

TO: Superintendent, Greenwood Elementary School District
FROM: Director, Curriculum and Instruction, GESD
DATE: May 14
RE: Planning for implementation of state standards

With the state's refusal to grant a waiver or a delay of implementation of the new state Department of Education Curriculum Standards, we must now make specific plans for what will be required for the implementation of these standards. I suggest that at the next Superintendent's Council, we place on the agenda the specific items that we must address in meeting the state mandate. The members of our council, consisting of district and school administrators, and teacher and community representatives, could provide valuable insight.

I know you will want to share the agenda items with the board of education, so the board members can be informed of our efforts to comply with the state mandate and still preserve local control over the excellent educational programs of the district. I am prepared to brief the council, and the board, if appropriate, of the instructional implications of the new state mandate.

## Module III: Analysis of Information and Decision Making

The five exercises in the Analysis of Information and Decision Making module are scored on a three-point scale, with 2 the highest possible score and 0 the lowest. The response to the two questions associated with each document are treated as a single response for scoring purposes, so only one score is assigned to each document.

### Sample Exercise

Read the document that follows and answer the following two questions:

From the point of view of a superintendent, describe at least three essential elements of effective communication.

Identify and explain at least three steps the superintendent could take to develop programs, techniques, and channels for implementing this policy.

Birch Grove Public School District<br>
Policy<br>
Concepts and Roles in Community Relations: Goals and Objectives

The board of education believes that school district–community relations should consist not solely of an information program, but should encompass all aspects of the schools' relationship with the total community.

The board of education believes its school–community relations program should:

1. Promote public interest and participation in the operation of the school system;
2. Gather information about public attitudes toward the school system and its programs and report them to the superintendent and the board;

3.  Provide an honest, continuous, comprehensive flow of information about the policies, procedures, programs, problems and progress of the school system to the community and the staff;
4.  Develop the most effective means of communication with the school system's public audience and use available media as appropriate;
5.  Develop programs in the school that will integrate home, school, and community in meeting the needs of district pupils;
6.  Develop and maintain the confidence of the community in the school board and the school staff;
7.  Develop a climate that attracts good teachers and encourages staff to strive for excellence in the educational program;
8.  Anticipate and forestall problems that are brought about by lack of understanding;
9.  Evaluate past procedures in order to make improvements in future communications.

The superintendent shall be responsible for developing programs, techniques, and channels for implementing this policy.

*Relevant ISLLC Standards*

Standards 1 and 4

*General Scoring Guide*

The following general scoring guide is used to score all responses in the Analysis of Information and Decision Making module.

*Score: 2.* A score of 2 presents a well-developed analysis or interpretation of the document based on a clear understanding and application of the underlying standards. A typical response in this category:

*   demonstrates a clear understanding of the standards applicable to the document and its interpretation or analysis;
*   applies the appropriate standards in a manner that is consistent with the intent and spirit of the standards;
*   clearly identifies and analyzes the relevant information, concepts, and/or issues presented in the document;
*   provides clear and specific answers to both questions and supports the answers with specific examples from the documents; and
*   provides a logical and reasonable rationale for answers when requested.

*Score: 1.* A score of 1 presents an analysis or interpretation of the document based on a general understanding and application of the underlying standards, but may also be uneven in its presentation. A typical response in this category:

- demonstrates a general understanding of the standards applicable to the document and its interpretation or analysis;
- applies the standards in a manner that is supportive of the intent and spirit of the standards;
- generally identifies and analyzes the important information, concepts, and/ or issues presented in the document;
- provides a general or uneven answer to one or both questions and/or provides general support with examples from the documents; and
- provides an acceptable rationale for answers when requested.

*Score: 0.* A score of 0 may demonstrate some competence in interpreting or analyzing the document, but is clearly limited or flawed. A typical response in this category:

- demonstrates a weak understanding of the standards applicable to the document and its interpretation or analysis;
- does not apply appropriate standards or applies standards in opposition to the intent and spirit of the standards;
- overlooks important relevant information in the document and/or seriously misinterprets or misunderstands the information, concepts, and/or issues presented in the document;
- provides a vague, inappropriate, or illogical answer to the question or fails to provide any support for the answer provided; and
- provides an inappropriate or illogical rationale or does not provide a rationale when one is requested.

## CONCLUSION

In chapter 7, the nature of the SLLA is described. Sample multiple-choice items and constructed-response items are presented from ETS's web link. The scoring guides and sample responses are included. We have referenced several times that there have been multiple versions of SLLA. Included in chapter 7 are sample vignettes based on other versions of SLLA. Also, sample modules from the Superintendent's Assessment are included.

# NOTES

1.  Educational Testing Service. (2009). A Study Guide for the School Leaders Licensure Assessment (SLLA). Retrieved from www.ets.org/Media/Tests/SLS/pdf/1011.pdf.

2.  Educational Testing Service. (2009). A Study Guide for the Superintendent's Assessment. Retrieved from www.ets.org/Media/Tests/SLS/pdf/1020.pdf.

*Chapter Eight*

# Case Studies Linked to ISLLC Standards and Conclusion

## Gregg Stall and Obie Cleveland Hill

Case studies have been used in many sectors of education for decades for the purposes of providing the equivalent of field-based or authentic experiences for candidates to utilize concepts and principles. The case studies in chapter 8 may also be used in preparation for the examination and for in-class discussions with aspiring leaders and teachers. The cases are based on practical experiences of both Dr. Stall and Dr. Hill. Dr. Stall is a department head in a regional institution in Louisiana with thirty years of experience over a wide range of educational environments; Dr. Hill is a retired dean of a college of education with over thirty-five years in education. For each case, ISLLC standards and questions for consideration are provided.

The authors strongly suggest that candidates for school and district administration licensure form small study groups and apply the ISLLC standards when developing decision strategies as they progress through the case studies. However, candidates are cautioned that there is no one specific solution in any of the cases. We take the position that if candidates diligently apply the standards to the case studies; this is a good preparation.

CASE 1

**Preparing for a New Leadership Role**

*ISLLC Standard(s) Considered*: 1, 2, 3, 4, and 5

*Case Scenario*: Karl Jones is still ecstatic over his appointment as the new principal at Jonestown Middle School. There is still a month to go before he will actually begin the job and two and one-half months before the school year starts. This appointment will be Karl's first principal's position, although he served as an assistant principal at the other middle school in Jonestown.

Bob Smith is the person Karl is replacing. Bob had been principal for the twelve previous years. He inherited a school that had one of the lowest performance ratings in the state. From 1999 until 2009 Jonestown Middle School had experienced steady, measureable growth in student performance as determined by increased standardized test scores and reduced student absences.

When Bob Smith had arrived at Jonestown, the school performance score was 36; the percentage of students successfully passing their state assessment tests was 31 percent; and on an average, only 41 percent of the students enrolled attended school each day. By 2009; the school performance score was 84 percent, with 77 percent of students passing state assessment tests and average daily attendance at 91 percent. However, after ten years of consistent gains, percentages on all three metrics had declined two consecutive years.

Karl Jones's charge upon appointment was simple: reverse the trend! He already had some ideas he was prepared to implement. However, as he prepared plans and strategies to implement his ideas, an incident occurred at his former school that awakened him to another reality. Simply put, that reality is: school leaders charged with school reform and turnaround have to be prepared to deal with unexpected problem issues, especially in the absence of policies that cover those issues.

Although he did not have all of the details, Karl Jones had these facts about the incident that took place at his former school. An eighth-grade student there had used his smart phone to download and forward pornographic material to ten of his friends. Several of those friends in turn forwarded the material to their friends, and before anyone knew what was happening 89 percent of the sixth-, seventh-, and eighth-grade students at the school had received and saved the porn material on their personal electronic devices, including smart phones and personal computers.

As soon as the principal of Karl's former school became aware of the incident, he enlisted the help of Jonestown City Police and confiscated the smart phones and personal computers of all the students who had them at school. Karl had no other information. The only policy in place at the school forbade students to use school computers to view or download any illicit material. What surprised Karl Jones the most, however, and as reported on the local television station, was not the fact that middle-school students were viewing porn material; the biggest surprise was the large number of parents objecting to the confiscation of their children's electronic devices.

Karl Jones was preparing to implement reform and turnaround measures at his new school. However, he could not help reflecting on how he would approach such an incident at his new school if there was no school or district policy to address it. He reasoned, "My reform initiative now must be forward thinking to the extent of developing school policies that, driven by rapid changes in technology, are general and comprehensive enough to encompass such unexpected incidents."

*Questions*: With reference to the ISLLC standards cited above and only the incidents at Karl's old school:

1. Which types of knowledge and understanding are required for the administrator/school leader to address this case? List at least five and justify each one chosen.
2. Which dispositions are required for the administrator/school leader to address this case? List at least five and justify each one chosen.
3. Which performance indicators should the administrator/school leader apply in this case? List at least five and justify each one chosen.
4. If you were Karl Jones, what steps would you take to develop a general technology policy comprehensive enough to cover the next five years?

## CASE 2

### Defining Cheating

*ISLLC Standard(s) Considered*: 2 and 5

*Case Scenario*: John Sally has been nervously pacing the floor of his study since midnight. He knows that he has to be ready for school in three hours, and he would welcome some sleep. He also knows that at ten o'clock later that morning he has to attend a hearing with the district superintendent and his staff and decide whether two of his teachers will be dismissed due to accusations of cheating.

John Sally is in his twelfth year as a high-school principal. He remembers well the advent of the school accountability movement. It began when he was an assistant principal. He remembers the subsequent introduction of high-stakes testing for determining whether students would be promoted to a higher grade and/or graduate from high school. He also knows that more and more student achievement as measured by standardized tests will play a major role in teacher and school leader evaluations. His school, like all others in his state, remains under constant pressure to improve test scores, meet mandated school performance scores, and decrease dropout numbers.

Over the course of the twelve years he has been principal, his high school has displayed rapid improvement, followed by stagnation, then slow growth, and over the past two years rapid growth again. Never in his wildest imagination, however, would he have thought the recent rapid growth was attributed in part to possible cheating, especially by two of his best teachers. It is now 5:30 a.m. John Sally has given up on getting any sleep. He decides to shower and get dressed for school and for that dreaded 10:00 a.m. hearing.

The hearing began promptly at 10:00 a.m. The superintendent called everyone to order and, after announcing the names of everyone in attendance, asked his deputy superintendent to read the charges against the two teachers. The deputy superintendent stated the following: "Amy Smith, a tenth-grade English teacher, and Alice Smith, no relation, a tenth-, eleventh-, and twelfth-grade mathematics teacher, have been charged with changing responses on answer sheets for the students they monitored during last spring's state-mandated testing."

After the charges were read, the superintendent allowed the teachers to respond to them. Amy Smith made this statement: "Madam Superintendent, Alice Smith and I work very closely together in helping our students prepare for annual testing, and with respect to time, I will allow her to speak for me."

Alice Smith began and offered this short statement: "Madame Superintendent and other members present, the current state school law says that it is forbidden for any teacher, during the course of state-mandated testing, to give any student answers to test questions; to coach a student to the correct answer; or to change students' responses after the test is completed. I state unequivocally that neither Amy Smith nor I ever engaged in such practices. However, I will say that we have gotten copies of old standardized tests, changed some of the details and numbers in some of the problems, and used these materials to drill our students.

"This is, in all honesty, teaching to the test, and we find it morally repugnant. However, under present state law and district policy, we have not committed any violations. As long as standardized testing is used to determine whether a student is promoted or graduates, and as these tests are more and more used to determine how teachers are evaluated, then measures such as ours that fall just outside of violations of the law and policy will occur."

After statements had been made by the teachers, the superintendent, John Sally, and other school district authorities, a committee was assigned to determine whether or not violations had been made by Amy and Alice Smith. The committee was made up of two other teachers, the curriculum supervisor, the deputy superintendent, and the president of the Parent Teacher Organization (PTO). John Sally was tasked to be a member of the committee to offer advice but not vote on the outcome.

*Questions*: With reference to the ISLLC standards cited above, if you were John Sally and you had to decide the outcomes of this hearing:

1. Which types of knowledge and understanding would you require as an administrator/school leader in this case? List at least five and justify each.
2. Which dispositions do you think you need as an administrator/school leader in addressing this case? List at least five and justify each.
3. Which performance indicators would you as an administrator/school leader apply in this case? List at least five and justify each.
4. Is the use of old testing material to drill students a form of cheating if there is no law/policy against it?

## CASE 3

### Implementing Value-Added Evaluation

*ISLLC Standard(s) Considered*: 1, 2, 3, 4, 5, and 6

*Case Scenario*: Jordan Thomas is entering his thirty-sixth year as an educator. He began his career as a high-school science and social studies teacher. After twelve years in the classroom, he was offered and accepted a position as an assistant principal at the same school. He remained an assistant principal for eight years and was then promoted to the job of principal. However, the setting for the new job was at one of the lowest-performing middle schools in the district. After thirteen years as a middle-school principal, he decided to complete his studies for a higher degree. Over the past two years, he has been on sabbatical leave completing the requirements for the doctoral degree in educational administration and leadership. As he prepares to return to the district, he recently learned that he would not be returning to a principal's position but instead to a role as a curriculum supervisor.

During his tenure as a middle-school principal, Mr. Thomas implemented reforms that resulted in his school moving from the lowest-performing in the district to the highest-performing one and also into the top 10 percent of middle schools in the state. Mr. Thomas was often called a student- and teacher-centered leader. The reforms he instituted and the methods he used to implement them often reflected this characterization. As a school administrator and leader, Jordan Thomas seemed to be everywhere and hands-on involved in everything. He never hesitated to delegate duties. He empowered his teachers to become school leaders in their own right.

When teacher empowerment was rarely practiced, Mr. Thomas was already putting innovations in place that required close collaborations and cooperation. He and his faculty started a before-school breakfast initiative; they implemented an extended-day academic program; cooperative learning ventures were developed and became featured curricula strategies; student-led leadership councils were developed; extensive parental involvement strategies were started, nurtured, and became integral to the mission of the school; and technology was heavily infused into the classrooms and academic instructional labs.

In his last year as the school's principal, his institution had become the top middle school in the district and in the top 10 percent in the state. All of this occurred despite having a student population in which 73 percent received free and reduced-price lunches. As a high-poverty school, Jordan Thomas and his teachers never allowed this statistic to deter their march toward excellence.

Mr. Thomas now prepares to assume his role as secondary curriculum supervisor. He has embraced his new role. However, in this new role he has been appointed as the committee chair charged with implementing a value-added evaluation system for the purpose of assessing teacher and administrator effectiveness. It is in his role as committee chair that he has trepidations. The trepidations are rooted in Jordan Thomas's beliefs about how to implement reforms and the long time it takes for these reforms to begin to show results.

His committee has to develop a system in which teachers and administrators will be evaluated in two years and in which the state mandates that 50 percent of the evaluations be based on students' performances on standardized test scores. The other 50 percent will be based upon other metrics that Mr. Thomas's committee must develop. Several questions trouble Jordan Thomas: How do you develop common assessments for teachers and administrators? How do you adequately measure such intangibles as collegiality, collaboration skills, and the ability to cooperate? Who should perform the evaluations—teachers of principals, principals of teachers, or combinations?

The district developmental evaluation team is composed of the secondary schools curriculum supervisor (Mr. Thomas), the elementary schools curriculum supervisor, three principals (one each from an elementary, middle, and high school), and three teachers (same composition). The superintendent informed the committee that other members could be added at their discretion. The task is straightforward: develop quantitative and qualitative criteria that will make up 50 percent of the value-added metrics for teacher and school-site administrator evaluations.

*Questions*: With reference to the ISLLC standards cited above:

1. Which types of knowledge and understanding should the committee consider? Cite at least three from each standard chosen.
2. Which dispositions should the committee consider? Cite at least three from each standard chosen.
3. Which performance indicators should the committee use as metrics? Cite at least three from each standard chosen.
4. What other persons should be added to the committee? Why?

5. What are some intangibles that do not lend themselves well to measurement but nonetheless, in your opinion, should be included in any value-added evaluation system?

## CASE 4

### Addressing a Sudden Cultural/Climate Shift

*ISLLC Standard(s) Considered*: 1, 2, 3, 4, 5, & 6

*Case Scenario*: Stall Elementary, a Pre-K–4 school, has had the luxury of an experienced school leader for ten years. Mr. Greggs worked in Stallston district for over twenty-five years, with fifteen years as a teacher and ten years as a school leader. He was appointed as school leader from the ranks of the classroom, which is a rare occurrence in his district. Prior to becoming principal, Greggs was a fourth-grade teacher at Stall Elementary. The school has a population of 550 students, with 60 percent African American and 40 percent white.

Greggs has been recognized in the district numerous times for his exceptional teaching abilities; within the past academic year, Greggs was named "Principal of the Year" in the district. Greggs is also known as an instructional leader throughout the district. He conducts many informal observations and works with teachers to facilitate professional development. There are ten schools in Stallston, with a population of five thousand students in Stallston; there are several parochial schools; and the percentage of students being homeschooled has increased.

Stall is the largest elementary school in Stallston and is the highest-performing school. The school performance score is among the higher performance scores in the state, and the school has a reputation of being an academics-oriented school. Parents are actively involved in parent-teacher groups, and students and parents have a sense of pride and ownership in the school. Annually, Stall Elementary has a fall festival. The single event provides a profit of twenty-five thousand dollars to the school; much of the work is done by parents. Fund-raising has been critical to the success of several innovative programs.

Traditionally, the parents have sponsored and organized the fall festival. Stall has experienced four retirements within the past academic year, and four beginning teachers have been added to the staff. The beginning teachers are recent graduates of the teacher education program near Stallston. The university has a good working relationship with the district. The new teachers were excited about the fall festival and asked Mr. Greggs to participate with the parents in the organization.

Mr. Greggs agreed to allow the beginning teachers to participate with the organization of the fall festival and called a meeting with the parent volunteers to begin the planning. Initially, it appeared to be a good plan, and it seemed the parents and new teachers would work well together. The teachers began using their planning times to organize activities and supplies for the festival. Other teachers were displeased with the notion that teachers were allowed to use their planning times for planning of the fall festival activities. Parents were informed of the situations and were also displeased.

Before the complaint was formally discussed with Mr. Greggs from the teachers at the school, he received a call from his immediate supervisor at the central office informing him of the complaint. Teachers from Stall had phoned the central office to register the complaint. Mr. Greggs called two additional meetings. One meeting was with the committee that was planning the fall festival. He informed them of the complaint and that he received a call from the central office. Mr. Greggs took the beginning teachers off of the committee for fall festival. The second meeting was with the faculty, in which Mr. Greggs discussed the complaint from the central office, but he also mentioned his disappointment with the teachers for not discussing the matter with him before filing a complaint with the central office.

Within a few days, Mr. Greggs noticed that several teachers were sitting behind desks during instructional time; teachers were arriving late to school; teachers appeared discontent; several teachers requested transfers; and it appeared that the climate had rapidly plummeted. Given all the factors in the case, how does Mr. Greggs address the climate? How will this impact achievement in the school?

*Questions*: With reference to the ISLLC standards cited above, what should Mr. Greggs consider?

1. Which types of knowledge and understanding are required for the administrator/school leader to address this case? List at least five and justify each one chosen.
2. Which dispositions are required for the administrator/school leader to address this case? List at least five and justify each one chosen.
3. Which performance indicators should the administrator/school leader apply in this case? List at least five and justify each one chosen.
4. If you were Mr. Stall, would you have had a different plan from the meetings?

CASE 5

## Ensuring Academic Integrity

*ISLLC Standard(s) Considered*: 2 and 5

*Case Scenario*: Hilly High School is the only high school in Kenny district; there are about 1,200 students in grades 9–12. Hilly has a mixture of experienced and inexperienced teachers. Mr. Obie is in his third year as school leader, and the district experienced several major initiatives since his assuming the role—the elementary and middle schools were restructured as linked to grade-level configurations with some rezoning; the district adopted mathematics and reading initiatives; and the district has adopted a new model for meeting the needs of special-needs students.

Kenny district has also experienced several leadership shifts. The superintendent is in her second year, and half of the central office staff has retired. Furthermore, most of the school leaders have been reassigned at the request of the school board. The superintendent and central office staff have been promoting the philosophy of site-based management and budgeting, providing the opportunities for the school leaders to have additional autonomy.

Mr. Obie is a huge advocate of professional learning communities. One of the activities addressed for several school improvement goals for Hilly High School is professional learning communities. Mr. Obie feels that this is one way to achieve and sustain academic growth in high schools. Hilly is departmentalized, like most high schools in the region, and teachers in the same departments have common planning. In addition, there are professional development activities where teachers plan with colleagues in different disciplines.

Mr. Obie has also encouraged teachers to supplant instruction with technology. Many of the students at Hilly have access to technology. Some of the classes are web-based classes for students who attend school for half of the day; the faculty members also embrace this notion because it grants them freedom. In one of the professional learning community meetings, one of the more experienced teachers, Ms. Apple, shared with the staff that one of her courses is listed as a traditional course, but the course is held during the last hour of the day, and she allows students to leave the campus and complete the work online.

Mr. Obie is made aware of the situation with the online versus "face-to-face" challenges and conferences with Ms. Apple about it. Ms. Apple informs Mr. Obie that she does not see a problem with providing students the option because it is the last hour of the day and students are performing exceptionally well in the applied mathematics course. Ms. Apple has been teaching at the school for about five years, with mediocre ratings. However, she has twenty years of teaching experiences in mathematics. What course of action should Mr. Obie take?

*Questions*: With reference to the ISLLC standards cited above, what should Mr. Obie consider?

1. Which types of knowledge and understanding are required for the administrator/school leader to address this case? List at least five and justify each one chosen.
2. Which dispositions are required for the administrator/school leader to address this case? List at least five and justify each one chosen.
3. Which performance indicators should the administrator/school leader apply in this case? List at least five and justify each one chosen.
4. If you are Mr. Obie, would you require the teacher to meet with the last-hour class? Why or why not?


CASE 6


## Competing Needs for Funding

*ISLLC Standard(s) Considered*: 1, 3, and 4

*Case Scenario*: Eugene High School is a rural high school in a small district with a rather unique situation. Over 75 percent of the teachers and nearly 100 percent of the staff are graduates of the high school. In addition, most of the parents are graduates of the high school, and over 50 percent of the parents are professionals. The parents are also active in the school community and embrace the need for a college preparatory curriculum. The parents support the school financially through many fund-raisers and have an active alumni association.

Mr. Kennedy served as school leader at Eugene High for over twenty years; he was also a product of the high school and district. The superintendent faced a dilemma in replacing Mr. Kennedy because there were only three applicants for the principalship. The most qualified applicant was not employed by the district; and the superintendent recommended the "out-of-district applicant" over two "in-house applicants." There were initially school and community relations challenges. However, the challenges were over in a few weeks.

In his first year, Dr. Hamilton took time to become familiar with the data at Eugene High School. He conducted a thorough needs analysis and involved teachers in school improvement planning, adopting a revised vision. The community was excited about the process because many community leaders and parents participated. The district had a surplus of funding and allocated a significant amount of the funding to Eugene High School for addressing curriculum.

There were funds previously allocated for a computer lab, and Dr. Hamilton felt that the lab was needed as revealed through the needs assessment data. Dr. Hamilton also felt the need to allocate a large percentage of the surplus funding from the district for vocational training for students. Both the teachers and parents are in disagreement with the allocation of funding to the vocational training. The parents and teachers feel like the surplus funding should be allocated to developing a second computer lab or for providing additional college preparatory courses. The alumni parent group has requested a meeting with Dr. Hamilton.

*Questions*: With reference to the ISLLC standards cited above, what should Dr. Hamilton consider?

1. Which types of knowledge and understanding are required for the administrator/school leader to address this case? List at least five and justify each one chosen.
2. Which dispositions are required for the administrator/school leader to address this case? List at least five and justify each one chosen.
3. Which performance indicators should the administrator/school leader apply in this case? List at least five and justify each one chosen.
4. If you were Dr. Hamilton, how would you prepare for the meeting?

CASE 7

**Everyone's Happy**

*ISLLC Standard(s) Considered*: 1, 2, 3. 4, 5, and 6

*Case Scenario*: As Graham Jacobs again reviewed the bundle of information and countless accountability files handed down to him when he entered his office for the first time, it all became very clear to him. Jacobs had been away for several years after growing up in this small southern city. Although being appointed principal of the district's largest middle school was a significant step down from his past administrative and supervisory positions at one of the most successful and prestigious school districts in the state, Jacobs felt that he was near the end of his career and wished to retire in his hometown and be close to his elderly parents.

Besides, Jacobs anticipated that the job would not be very demanding due to the fact that little had changed in his hometown since he departed to attend the university decades before. He was familiar with most of the teachers at the school, having attended school with them or a close relative of theirs.

Several of them were actually close friends of his with whom he lost touch after opting to attend the state's flagship university as opposed to the small university located thirty-five miles away.

Although test scores at the school were somewhat stagnant, they were far too average to draw any negative attention. School disciplinary records painted a rosy picture in that Summit Hills Middle School recorded below-average numbers of referrals and just one expulsion hearing in past five years. Likewise, attendance rates showed fairly average to slightly above-average attendance rates. Summit Hills was the sole feeder school for Summit Hills High School, one of the district's two high schools.

Although Summit Hills test scores were simply mediocre, the school regularly garnished higher accountability scores than its district counterpart. The one area where both schools were significantly below state average was in the high dropout rate. The availability of menial jobs at the plants dulled many concerns in this area since there were employment opportunities for those who did not complete school.

While a fairly low percentage of the students completing high school pursued a postsecondary education, the community reaped the benefits of having two large national fabrication plants in the area. Plant management officials often praised the local school system for providing an adequate workforce for the plants. There always were more than enough jobs, even for those students who failed to complete high school.

What concerned Mr. Jacobs was that as he walked the science hall, he noticed that while the school was somewhat ethnically and economically diverse, the classes were not. When peeking in on the advanced chemistry class working in the lab, he realized that most of the college preparatory classes were made up of mainly upper-middle-class to upper-class white kids, while vocational or noncollege prep classes were more inclusive. What further concerned Mr. Jacobs was that the special education classes, which were still operated as self-contained classrooms, were predominately made up of lower-income students, most of them Hispanic or black students.

When Mr. Jacobs shared his observations with Mr. Kenny, his childhood friend, long-term Summit Hills faculty member and recently appointed assistant principal, Mr. Kenny chuckled and commented, "You've been away too long; this is the way it's always been." "Besides," Mr. Kenny went on, "it works best that way. Every teacher can tailor her instruction to meet the students' needs. By doing it this way, we have fewer discipline problems because the teachers can teach at each student's level." Mr. Kenny then went on to cite disciplinary statistics and proudly boasted that if it were not for a few of the lower-end academic classes and the special education classes, the school would have virtually no disciplinary problems at all.

"Besides," Mr. Kenny boasted, "academically, we're right where we should be." Mr. Jacobs did his best not to cringe when he heard this last statement, as this seemed to be the motto of all those he had dealt with since returning home, including the superintendent, teachers, plant supervisor, and parents. While just smiling and nodding in each of those past instances, this time he apparently could not contain himself, as he was as surprised as Mr. Kenny to hear "Et tu, Kenny," come from his own lips.

*Questions*: With reference to ISLLC standards, consider the following:

1. An argument could be made that the current climate of the school serves to meet the needs of the students and is simply responsive to the larger political, social, economic, legal, and cultural context of the community. Review standard 6 and the associated knowledge, dispositions, and performance and counter this argument.
2. As Mr. Jacobs ends his professional career, his most prudent course of action would be to simply stay the course and work to make subtle changes designed to improve test scores at the school. From a professional standpoint, discuss moral and ethical issues that warrant Mr. Jacobs's professional attention.
3. Based upon your work with questions 1 and 2, speculate on Mr. Jacobs's vision for the school.
4. Review standards 1 and 2 and then discuss the prerequisites to Mr. Jacobs's bringing about substantive changes to the culture at the school.

# CASE 8

## The Role of Management in Addressing School Climate

*ISLLC Standard(s) Considered*: 3 and 4

*Case Scenario*: Second Ward High School, located in a rural community in Louisiana, houses grades 7–12. The student population at the school is 704, with approximately 70 percent of the school classified as minority. The majority of the student body is economically at risk, with over 85 percent of the students being eligible for free or reduced-fee lunch. Traditionally, the Second Ward community is a very tight-knit community, with the school serving as a hub for many social and recreational activities. Parental involvement at the school can be described as very high, especially when it comes to athletics.

In spite of the active involvement of the community, conditions at the school leave a lot to be desired. Test scores have been very low and fairly stagnant for many years, and most teachers issue discipline referrals hourly.

Due to the rough working conditions for teachers, the turnover rate for teachers and staff is very high. In addition to the noted lack of discipline at the school, many teachers have grumbled about the lack of communication between administrators, teachers, and staff members.

The relationship between the school and the community took a turn for the worse when the football team, a traditional powerhouse, had two losing seasons in a row. The school district decided to make drastic changes to the school leadership by removing both the principal and the coach and replacing each with an outsider to the community. This certainly was not the norm. What made manners even more tense was the fact that the school system replaced the coach with little community input.

In addition to Mr. O'Brien being the new school principal, there were ten new teachers at the school to start the new school year. Most of these teachers were first-year teachers. Mr. O'Brien welcomed these new teachers as he felt that the school obviously needed a fresh start. Mr. O'Brien is a positive, upbeat person and is motivated to make changes. He is coming into the school with new ideas and wants to be a successful leader.

In assessing the situation at Second Ward, Mr. O'Brien was most concerned with the school culture. Morale at the school was low for some time, and people spoke openly about the tyrannical leadership style of his predecessor. After just a few weeks into the school year, he quickly realized that his job was going to be tougher than he thought. He was bombarded with many parental complaints as the school football team was dismally defeated in the first three ball games of the season.

Furthermore, during these visits, parents complained at length about teachers, class discipline, and the difficulties they faced in getting their kids to attend school. These were issues Mr. O'Brien understood to be moot points prior to the "football" fiasco. Interestingly, the majority of these educational concerns involved the middle-school students at the school rather than the high-school students.

Mr. O'Brien prepared himself for the worst when Coach Gros, a middle-aged assistant coach and veteran teacher at the school, asked to meet with him in private. He thought, "Here it is, my first coaching defection . . . and a local guy at that. Could things be any worse?" To his shock, Coach Gros wanted to discuss his classes and the plight of middle-school students at the school. Coach Gros went on to point out that due to budget cuts, the district consolidated the two middle schools in the area and sent all of the seventh- and eighth-grade students to Second Ward High. Coach Gros pointed out that the middle schools had all of the frills, including football teams, homecoming dances, cheerleaders, and so on. The past principal was not at all happy with the district's decision, and he placed a premium on ensuring that the middle-school students housed at the school maintained a separate identity from the rest of the school. Although they had their own hallway, restrooms, and lunch period, they were given little else. Middle-school students were not allowed to attend high-school dances or pep rallies or to join the school's clubs. Coach Gros indicated that he understood the separation to some degree; however, he felt there was very little that the school offered to these students. Coach Gros felt that these policies affected the morale of both students and faculty at the entire school.

Immediately upon hearing Coach Gros's concerns, a light went on in Mr. O'Brien's head, and immediately he realized that he had fallen into the trap of being a reactive leader guilty of wearing blinders and dealing with the school's issues in isolation.

*Questions*: With reference to the ISLLC standards, consider the following questions:

1. Review standard 3 and discuss the managerial and operational facets of the school that can be changed in order to address several of the school's problems. Could such issues be related to addressing the "football issue?" Consider this issue from more than one perspective.
2. Procedurally, provide a possible "blueprint" for addressing the issues discussed in the scenario. For instance, after reviewing standard 4, what would you suggest as Mr. O'Brien's first course of action . . . and so on?
3. From a leadership perspective, what opportunities does this scenario provide for Mr. O'Brien's attempt to *change* the culture of the school? What is working in Mr. O'Brien's favor, and what are possible road-blocks?

## CONCLUSION

In chapter 5, the challenges in education associated with accountability were discussed, including some of the historical challenges and the current direction for education—many states are adopting the recently developed common core for the curriculum. Some states are also applying for waivers to be exempt from NCLB and reauthorization. The implications of/for the common core with assessment alignment were also discussed. Obviously, the roles of school leaders and teachers remain critical for school improvement.

In chapter 6, in the discussion of the ISLLC standards, the roles of school leaders are discussed pertinent to each standard with emphases to some extent on accountability. One monumental challenge that persists in education for all educators is the need for systemic reform with all stakeholders taking "radical responsibility" in the process. Because the focus of this volume is on the role of the leader, it is noteworthy to discuss Siccone's[1] (2012) points discussed in *Essential Skills for Effective School Leadership.*

As pertinent to school leadership; Siccone[2] (2012) suggests that school leaders must take "radical responsibility" to provide direction for school leadership. The following are the six rules aligned with radical responsibility:

1. Responsibility is fact finding, not fault finding.
2. Responsibility is acting purposefully.
3. Responsibility is the ability to respond appropriately.
4. Responsibility is using language that connotes power.
5. Responsibility is encouraging others to take appropriate action.
6. Responsibility is an internal sense of being empowered to act.

An important notion embedded in rule 1—responsibility is fact finding, not fault finding—is for the leader to analyze situations objectively. There is often minimal value in assigning blame to individuals. Actions that have been committed cannot be uncommitted. Keeping focused and moving forward becomes most valuable. Stone, Patton, and Heen[3] (1999) present how to discuss what matters most in their publication *Difficult Conversations.*

In every difficult situation as it relates to analyses, three conversations should occur—"what happened conversation; feelings conversation; and identity conversation." Assumptions can be very dangerous in progression forward as linked to discovering what actually occurred. Clarity in what occurred is essential. Validity of feelings and appropriateness of feelings are challenges for the feelings conversation, and the meaning debate is aligned with the identity conversation.

Siccone's[4] (2012) rule 2—responsibility is acting purposefully—aligns with clarity. The visions and missions of schools must be communicated effectively by school leaders with buy-in from all stakeholders. And the notion of clarity in communication pervades all dimensions of issues in schools and all other organizations. Hoy and Miskel[5] (2008) suggest that communication skills are essential to effective administration and cannot be isolated from decision making, motivating, and leading. The leader has to communicate the vision and high expectations for teaching and learning to promote positivism in cultures of schools. This premise was discussed as linked to instructional leadership and standard 2 of ISLLC.

Rule 3—responsibility is the ability to respond appropriately—requires school leaders to anticipate potential problems, develop contingency plans, and view obstacles as aligned with progress. The need to be proactive in comparison to reactive is applicable for leadership that permeates all work organizations as well as all sectors of society. However, there is an immediate need for school leaders to have some "foreseeability" when implementing initiatives in schools. Integrated in Siccone's rule 4—responsibility is using language that connotes power—is the need for the leader to exhibit confidence in his/her abilities. Siccone[6] (2012) suggests that word choices like "I'll try" or "I hope" are indicative of lower levels of ability or lower levels of commitment.

It is difficult to exemplify rule 5—responsibility is encouraging others to take appropriate action—when exhibiting low levels of commitment or low levels of ability. Implementation of rule 4 is a prerequisite for rule 5. It is always important for school leaders to direct individuals to the appropriate individuals and/or entities to address challenges. Some practitioners may disagree with this concept; however, parents (in most situations) should be directed to teachers when they present concerns or complaints about teachers to school leaders. And central office staff members and superintendents should not entertain complaints regarding school leaders (in most situations) without redirecting the individuals to the school leaders.

It is important for school leaders to make commitment levels public to ensure successful implementation of goals; this principle is aligned with Siccone's rule 6—responsibility is an internal sense of being empowered to act. School leaders should communicate what the measures of the goals are so that members of the school community are aware of the goals to assist in "raising the bar" for accountability.

In addition to rules, Siccone[7] (2012) presents five skills. As previously alluded to, the rules and skills discussed in Siccone's[8] (2012) *Essential Skills for Effective School Leadership* are aligned with the ISLLC standards discussed in chapter 6 of this volume: "ISLLC Standards and ELCC Standards." The five essential skills are confidence, communication, collaboration, coaching, and continuous improvement. Obviously, all of the skills are important. And confidence is embedded in the other four skills. Senge addresses the need for leaders to have confidence from the premise of Fullan's work.

Senge is cited in chapter 5; he wrote the foreword to Fullan's[9] (2010) *All Systems Go*. Senge says that Fullan has demonstrated that change is possible in K–12 schools, but it occurs through a systemic approach with a leader who has confidence. Kennedy[10] (2003) noted a similar assertion in *Raising Test Scores for All Students.* He said many of the reform efforts have been unsuccessful because they have been "fragmented." Therefore, change is possible, according to Fullan[11] (2010), and it starts with conviction and must be systemic, which is supported by other theorists and educational leaders including Kennedy[12] (2003).

There are varying philosophies and perspectives on what the real challenges are in K–12 schools as linked to the underperformance or lack of excellence in student performance. Senge[13] (2010) suggests that the real problem could be that too much effort has centered on a "one-size-fits-all" approach. Fullan (2010)[14] asserts a need for educators to believe change is possible; Kennedy [15] (2003) asserts that systemic reform should be the goal. There are many others who have shared perspectives in this area. However, regardless of perspectives and/or philosophies, we believe most educators will agree that school leaders and teachers are critical variables in moving schools forward. In the discussion in chapter 6, critical standards-based knowledge, skills, and dispositions for leaders in this era are presented with some emphases on accountability and instructional leadership.

In concluding, table 8.1 depicts three perspectives of critical variables for success in organizations.

The first column of table 8.1 includes the ten conditions of high-performing schools from Blase, Blase, and Phillips [16] (2010.) The second column includes the six characteristics of high-performing schools from Blankstein's [17] (2010) *Failure Is Not an Option*. The third column is from Darden Business School's 7-S Perspective of the *Leader's Guide to Understanding Complex Organizations*, originally developed by McKinsey.

| *Handbook*—Blase, Blase, & Phillips (2010) | *Failure Is Not an Option*— Blankstein (2010) | Darden Business School (UVA) 7-S Perspective |
| --- | --- | --- |
| Safe and orderly school environment | Common mission, vision, values, and goals | Strategy |
| Strong administrative leadership | Ensuring achievement for all students with systems for prevention and intervention | Structure |
| Primary focus on learning | Collaboration focused on teaching and learning | Systems |
| Maximizing learning time | Using data to guide decision making and continuous improvement | Superordinate goals |
| Monitoring student progress | Gaining active engagement from family and community | Style |
| Academically heterogeneous class assignments | Building sustainable leadership capacity | Staff (people) |
| Flexible in-class groups | | Skills |
| Small class size | | |
| Supportive classroom climate | | |
| Parent and community involvement | | |

Table 8.1. Three Perspectives of Critical Variables for Success in Organizations

Obviously, the focus in column three, developed by McKinsey,[18] is on businesses, while the focus for Blase, Blase, and Phillips[19] (2010) and Blankstein[20] (2010) is on schools. Amazingly, all three models target the role of the leader. Specifically, Blase, Blase, and Phillips[21] (2010) suggest that one of the characteristics of high-performing schools is strong administrative leadership while the other authors (presented in the table) have concepts that align with the need for strong leadership.

The role of the leader as an instructional leader was previously discussed as a component of ISLLC standards—specifically standard 2. Blase, Blase, and Phillips[22] (2010) suggest that the behavior of the leader impacts student achievement, which is linked to the important principles of instructional leadership. Furthermore, Marzano, Waters, and McNulty[23] (2005) suggest that there are many leadership dispositions and skills that impact student achievement. The largest variables are

- situational awareness (principal's awareness of details and occurrences in school and use of information to address problems);
- intellectual stimulation (principal's assurance of currency of theory and practices aligned with school culture);
- change agent (principal's challenging of status quo);
- input (principal's involvement of teachers in important decisions);
- culture (principal's fostering of shared beliefs and sense of community); and
- monitors/evaluates (principal's monitoring of practices and the impact on student learning).

Blankstein's[24] (2010) six characteristics of high-performing schools include the building of leadership capacity. Effective leaders "build cultures of leadership." It is difficult for an effective learning organization to function dependent on a single dynamic leader. Dynamic leaders empower others to lead. Embedded in both ISLLC standard 2 and ELCC standard 2 is the important role of the leader in building leadership capacity among the teaching staff. The capacity is developed through the leader building a positive culture and empowering staff.

As previously cited, the 7-S model presented in column 3 of table 8.1 was originally developed by McKinsey. The model was redesigned several times. In the most recent redesign from Pascale and Athos, they acknowledge the role of the leader as interrelated to all other components of the model. The leader is critical to success of businesses in the model. The models of Blankstein[25] (2010) and Blase, Blase, and Phillips [26] (2010) highlight the importance of leaders pertinent to instructional leadership.

The accountability movements linked to *A Nation at Risk*, NCLB, and the current reauthorization have all pinpointed the underperformance of students in K–12 schools. As previously cited, Siccone[27] (2010) suggests that the two single most important variables as linked to student achievement are teachers and principals. ISLLC and ELCC standards are presented in chapter 6 with a discussion to roles of school leaders. To meet the challenges of accountability, high-performing principals who are knowledgeable and who implement the skills and dispositions of the standards are critical to the profession.

## NOTES

1. Siccone, F. (2012). *Essential Skills for Effective School Leadership*. Boston: Pearson Education.
2. Ibid.
3. Stone, D., Patton, B., & Heen, S. (1999). *Difficult Conversations*. New York: Penguin.
4. Siccone, F. (2012). *Essential Skills for Effective School Leadership*. Boston: Pearson Education.
5. Hoy,W., & Miskel, C. (2008). *Educational Administration: Theory, Research, and Practice*. New York: McGraw-Hill.
6. Siccone, F. (2012). *Essential Skills for Effective School Leadership.*Boston: Pearson Education.
7. Ibid.
8. Ibid.
9. Fullan, M. (2010). *All Systems Go: The Change Imperative for Whole System Reform*. California: Corwin.
10. Kennedy, E. (2003). *Raising Test Scores for All Students: An Administrative Guide to Improving Standardized Test Performance*. California: Corwin.
11. Fullan, M. (2010). *All Systems Go: The Change Imperative for Whole System Reform*. California: Corwin.
12. Kennedy, E. (2003). *Raising Test Scores for All Students: An Administrator's Guide to Improving Standardized Test Performance*. California: Corwin.
13. Senge, P. (2010). Foreword to *All Systems Go: The Change Imperative for Whole System Reform*. California: Corwin.
14. Fullan, M. (2010). *All Systems Go: The Change Imperative for Whole System Reform*. California: Corwin.
15. Kennedy, E. (2003). *Raising Test Scores for All Students: An Administrator's Guide to Improving Standardized Tests Performance*. California: Corwin.
16. Blase, J., Blase, J., & Phillips, D. (2010). *Handbook of School Improvement: How High-Performing Principals Create High-Performing Schools*. California: Corwin.
17. Blankstein, A. (2010). *Failure Is Not an Option: 6 Principles for Making Student Success the Only Option*. California: Corwin.
18. McKinsey
19. Blase J., Blase, J., & Phillips, D. (2010). *Handbook of School Improvement: How High-Performing Principals Create High-Performing Schools*. California: Corwin.
20. Blankstein, A. (2010). *Failure Is Not an Option: 6 Principles for Making Student Success the Only Option*. California: Corwin.
21. Blase, J., Blase, J., & Phillips, D. (2010). *Handbook of School Improvement. How High-Performing Principals Create High-Performing Schools*. California: Corwin.
22. Ibid.
23. Marzano, R., Waters, T., & McNulty, B. (2005). *School Leadership That Works: From Research to Results*. Virginia: Association for Supervision and Curriculum Development.

24. Blankstein, A. (2010). *Failure Is Not an Option: 6 Principles for Making Student Success the Only Option.* California: Corwin.

25. Ibid.

26. Blase, J., Blase, J., & Phillips, D. (2010). *Handbook of School Improvement. How High-Performing Principals Create High-Performing Schools.* California: Corwin.

27. Siccone, F. (2012). *Essential Skills for Effective School Leadership.* Boston: Pearson Education.